SOCIAL POLICY & SOCIAL JUSTICE

Edited by
John L. Jackson, Jr.

Distributed for the University of Pennsylvania
School of Social Policy & Practice
by the University of Pennsylvania Press

PENN

UNIVERSITY OF PENNSYLVANIA PRESS

PHILADELPHIA

Distributed by
University of Pennsylvania Press
Philadelphia, Pennsylvania 19104-4112
www.upenn.edu/pennpress

Printed in the United States of America on acid-free paper
10 9 8 7 6 5 4 3 2 1

Library of Congress Cataloging-in-Publication Data
ISBN 978-1-5128-2146-8

CONTENTS

Social Policy
& Social Justice

INTRODUCTION

It's Not Just Social Policy,
It's Social Justice

John L. Jackson, Jr.

It should have been impossible. By some measures, it was a ludicrous idea. When HBO first launched in the early 1970s, there were so many reasons to bet against it.

For one thing, experts weren't totally sure if the technology that the entire business plan was to be built on—distant satellites beaming signals from outer space to television sets in cities and suburban enclaves all across the country—would actually work. Underground cables were one thing, but few people seemed willing or able to guarantee that those satellites would even stay in orbit, which meant taking out insurance policies specifically for the damage that might be done to unsuspecting people and their property if any of the metallic contraptions came careening back down to Earth.

Even if satellites didn't tumble out of the sky, there were still serious political and economic forces lined up against this fledgling endeavor. In fact, all the institutional supporters that HBO's executives would have needed in their corner seemed hell-bent on thwarting them. The movie studios wouldn't license them enough films. The major broadcast networks fought them tooth and nail. The Federal Communication Commission (FCC) just about outlawed their programming model in 1975. And as if all that weren't enough, HBO was being run by a magazine outfit, Time-Life, with no real television experience to speak of.

And none of those challenges rivaled what was maybe the most troubling thing of all: nobody was sure that enough people would ever be willing to *pay* for television, since they were used to getting it for free.

With that as backdrop, it wasn't a foregone conclusion that HBO would ever turn a profit, let alone become the media juggernaut it is today, but the company's early execs didn't let long odds stop them. Since the studios weren't supplying enough movies, HBO started making its own shows and relying on sports, especially boxing, to build the brand. Ali and Frazier's "Thrilla in Manila" was the first program HBO ever transmitted via satellite—though only two years before, in 1973, it was still airing polka festivals out of Pennsylvania. The FCC's antisiphoning decision, which limited the kind of programming HBO could offer, was declared unconstitutional by 1977. And those satellites never did rain down on people's heads!

For the smallest of the University of Pennsylvania's 12 schools, the School of Social Policy & Practice (SP2), colloquially known as Penn's Social Justice School, there are lessons to be learned from HBO's improbable story. It isn't just a trivialization to imagine that a media conglomerate might have something to teach policy makers and the people who train them about how to imagine an entirely new world into existence—against overwhelming odds and massive obstacles. And make no mistake about it, when talking about social justice, social policy, and social change, the odds are daunting, and the obstacles are undeniably real.

One challenge hinges on the difficulty of translating lofty concepts into everyday realities. Many of us can agree on ideals (freedom, equality, inclusion, fairness, patriotism, etc.) when they remain abstract and nonspecific, platitudes without particulars, but the moment we start to make those terms concrete, which is exactly what policy makers and activists do, our superficial agreements show signs of strain.

Partisanship in electoral politics is another challenge. So much of public culture is organized around zero-sum bloodsport that politicians tend to use a 24-hour news cycle and a never-ending electoral campaigning season to lob merciless and indiscriminant attacks at one another. Partisans aren't respecters of policy—much less justice. If the other side backs a reform or recommendation today, our side rejects it. Period. And that's even if we supported that same position at some point in the past. American politics today is both hyperideological and postideological at the same time. It is a world of unflinchingly committed neoliberals, neoconservatives, liberals, and progressives who are also usually willing to do whatever it takes to defeat the other side, political ideals be damned.

Maybe most important of all, American citizens have long held differing opinions about who legitimately belongs, about what being an *American* implies. We draw diverse—sometimes mutually exclusive—configurations of *us* and *them*, concentric circles of greater and lesser loyalty, of more or less empathy. Our policy priorities and our definitions of justice depend in part on the circumferences of those circles. All lives might matter, sure, but some of them matter more to us than others.

Immigration is only one of the most obvious examples of this political calculus, and our varied perspectives on relevant policies (such as mass deportation, pathways to citizenship, wall building along the southern border, safe haven cities, and religious bans on entry into the country) all provide working answers to the question of who we think *we* are. In a way, every single national election is a referendum on what it means to be American. On who counts. And it isn't just guided by the objective merits of a specific policy position. It is about how well we can communicate a policy's ethical and practical underbelly, what it declares about the scope of our legitimate social universe—a universe where certain people deserve our help and others deserve whatever they happen to get.

Every year, different issues come to the fore: welfare reform, mass incarceration, tax policy, policing. We are all asked to adhere to some single, coherent position. Should we, for example, "die-in" to protest the deadly consequences of a racialized criminal justice system, or do we dismiss such public demonstrations as stunts, little more than indications of antipolice and anti-American fanaticism?

Even the phrase "social justice" is contentious. Does it mean you are advocating for the redistribution of wealth? Or is it a way of making sure that the call for American individualism isn't rigged from the start? Reasonable people disagree. And then unreasonable ones contort those disagreements into massively dysfunctional and intractable civic conflagrations.

For portions of our body politic, even for some members of SP2, "social impact" or "social innovation" are more acceptable articulations of things than "social justice," though others dismiss such turns of phrase as examples of neoliberal naïveté. It is often hard to square those various philosophical/ideological positions, but SP2 faculty and students attempt to keep them in a productive tension similar to the kind that recognizes how both capital and Capitol Hill can be deployed, if mobilized thoughtfully, as positive catalysts for social change.

SP2 is Penn's smallest and least wealthy school, situated literally in the shadows of Wharton, one of the most globally recognized business brands in the world. Our school collaborates with Wharton on issues of social entrepreneurialism and research about effective philanthropy. We partner with Penn's nursing and education schools on research aimed at helping children and their families in as holistic and comprehensive a way as possible. In fact, we have collaborations with all of Penn's other schools. We are rabidly interdisciplinary, because the questions we want to answer, the problems most in need of solutions, can't be tackled from any single discipline.

I should point out that there are a few different reasons why the story of HBO is salient to me as I introduce the short and accessible essays in this volume. At SP2, we call our students (social workers, policy makers, and nonprofit leaders) "change agents," and change agents should be just as undaunted as those HBO execs were back in the early 1970s when they were willing to work toward their goals regardless of the high institutional, legal, and material barriers to success. For a relatively small school such as ours, it means not using our size as an excuse for setting goals that are anything other than ambitious and transformative.

The HBO example is also in my head because it just so happens that a group of Penn graduate students from SP2, the Annenberg School for Communication, and the School of Arts and Sciences have been working on a documentary about how the founding of HBO transformed television in the 1970s. But that isn't the end of the story. People can come up with subtle or dramatic ways to change their world, but they can never rest on their laurels. And HBO is an object lesson for that truth too. By some accounts, the satellite giant finds itself in danger of being HBO'd by other media innovators today. That 1970s upstart is now the big kid on the block, with streaming media services such as Netflix and Amazon Prime threatening to make its conventional subscription model obsolete.

Who knows what things will look like for the future of American television—let alone the future of American society? I can't predict what issues will demand major national reimagining in the years to come, and no scholarly expert has all the answers, but they are asking some of the necessary questions—sincerely, rigorously, and with an investment in positive social outcomes. This short book of essays represents one more example of that effort.

Ultimately, you have to decide for yourself what issues are most important to you. That is part of what democracy means. If you don't examine evidence carefully and ask enough questions, you can easily become a sucker to someone else's agenda. This is what makes democracy so demanding. The academic experts in this project are offering arguments about how we should envision our collective social policy/justice landscape as a function of research that they or their colleagues have conducted on crucial social issues. Some of these issues, such as gun control, are already mainstays of our national political conversation. Others (such as debates about how best to care for our youngest and most vulnerable citizens) probably deserve a lot more election-time discussion than they currently receive.

Some of the issues that trouble me most as an academic administrator in the 21st century (the current and ever-rising price tag for college and graduate school along with a growing demonization of the professoriate as left-wing ideologues brainwashing America's young) don't get extended treatment here, but they are high on my own list. And I don't just want to gather evidence on such topics to reinforce my current take on things; I especially need to know when my working assumptions are wrong—and why.

So, don't read these pieces as gospel, as definitive claims about what issues you absolutely have to privilege or how you *must* think about them. Instead, the facts, figures, theories, and opinions offered up are meant to represent some of the evidence already at your disposal on issues that impact your life and the lives of those you care about. You don't have to agree with all the authors' conclusions. You don't even have to accept many of their premises. You won't. But you should take up their challenge to assemble all the data, expertise, and historical context you can muster to make sense of the issues that matter most to you. As you read these essays, please know that this manuscript only succeeds if it can help in the ongoing impulse to get us all thinking a little more critically, a little more carefully, and a little more creatively about how to make sense of our world while positively transforming it.

Acknowledgments

Thank you to Steven Feldman for giving us the idea for both this short volume and the Penn Top Ten website www.penntopten.com. Also, a special thank you to Tamara Nopper, who worked with the authors on multiple drafts of their essays.

CHAPTER 1

Ending Homelessness Now

Dennis P. Culhane

On January 5, 2015, Mayor Mitch Landrieu of New Orleans announced that his city had *ended* veteran homelessness. According to the press announcement, not a single veteran remained among the city's homeless population. A year earlier, the city and its federal and community partners had generated a list of the nearly 200 homeless veterans in New Orleans and laid out a plan to house them one by one through a variety of programs. The news of this success made headlines, as did the proclamations a year earlier by the mayors of Phoenix and Salt Lake City that they too had ended chronic homelessness among veterans in their communities. These successes, perhaps unprecedented in any recent social policy arena, have demonstrated that concerted efforts by communities, in partnership with the federal government, can make a real and lasting difference for what was once a seemingly intractable social problem. These achievements have proven that the United States is poised to make even more compelling and dramatic improvements in the lives of some of the most vulnerable Americans by ending homelessness—among veterans *and* nonveterans—once and for all.

Ending homelessness in the United States is possible and within reach. Over the last several years homelessness has been declining, including among veterans and people who experience chronic homelessness. This decline is due to a change in long-standing practices among policy makers. The success of current homelessness policy can be attributed to greater reliance on evidence-based practices. Advocates, policy makers (including Congress and Presidents Barack Obama and George W. Bush), and practitioners in the field are to be credited with committing themselves to data-driven decision making rather developing policies based on stereotypes about homeless people. With further strategic investments, these policies can be *taken to scale*, and homelessness can become a thing of the past.

Longitudinal Research Establishes Scope and Dynamics of Homelessness

Research conducted in the early 1990s found that homelessness was more common than previously thought. Previous research had focused on single-night counts that, given the limited time frame, would be expected to yield a low count relative to most other methods. In 1994 two studies produced *longitudinal* estimates of homelessness for the first time, showing the cumulative impact of homelessness over a year or more rather than just on one given night. One study found that people responding to a household survey of the general U.S. population reported that 3.2% had stayed in an emergency shelter or slept in a place not meant for habitation for at least one night in the previous five years. A study of New York City's and Philadelphia's computerized shelter tracking systems yielded counts of the unique number of people to stay in a shelter in those cities, confirming that 3.2% had used those shelters in the previous five years, including 1% of each city's general population in 1992 alone. Adjusting for race and poverty, later studies established that as many as 25% of poor African American men in their 30s and 40s experienced homelessness in New York City in just 1995.

That homelessness could affect so many persons indicated that the problem was not only more widespread than previously thought but was also much more brief and episodic in nature. Such volumes of people could not be accommodated by these systems if there wasn't substantial turnover—people exiting the condition as well as entering. Researchers have since looked at the dynamics of homelessness using shelter records and have consistently found that indeed, as many as 75–80% of adults and families who use shelters do so on a relatively short-term basis, less than 60 to 90 days, a condition that could be called "crisis homelessness." Others either move in and out of shelters frequently over time or get stuck in the homelessness system for years on end in a condition called "chronic homelessness." Having identified these distinct patterns, research has further indicated that compared to people experiencing crisis homelessness, adults who experience chronic homelessness and families who are repeatedly homeless have much higher rates of behavioral health problems and disabilities and much higher intensive social support needs, such as child protection interventions for families.

Together, this evidence has helped to establish that a two-pronged approach to homelessness is needed, with strategies differentially targeting those who experience crisis homelessness and those who experience chronic homelessness.

Evidence-Based Programs Match Housing and Services with Need

Chronic Homelessness

People with severe mental disorders were among the first to argue that they needed and wanted normalized housing—housing as housing—not residential treatment programs, group homes, shelters, or transitional housing. Their self-advocacy led to the development of a housing model called "supported housing." As initially conceived, the housing was to come from the standard rental market, with the psychosocial support services acting as the "wheel-chair ramp" to help people obtain a unit, move in, and maintain the unit. The housing would not be a treatment program; it would be housing. But as service professionals in the homelessness sector began to experiment with this approach, it gradually morphed into supportive housing.

It was often in congregate nonprofit buildings (not in the standard rental market), which sometimes included treatment requirements or even sobriety, and included on-site treatment staff—effectively transmuting into what can sometimes look and feel like a residential treatment program.

Yet the model still seems to work, and throughout the 1990s efforts to place people who were chronically homeless into supportive housing saw great successes. But the more programmed the housing, the harder it was to place people who were stubbornly homeless, whose active substance use or resistance to treatment made them "hard to house," at least in the view of the programmed housing sector. In response, the Housing First approach emerged. Early innovators, such as Pathways to Housing in New York City, returned to the roots of the *supported* housing movement by self-advocates arguing that housing should just be housing, without treatment or sobriety requirements and in normal, standard rental units, with treatment independent of the housing. They proved that such an approach worked to stabilize even the so-called hard to house.

Thus, by 2002 the homelessness practice and policy field had identified a set of housing solutions for virtually all of the people who experience chronic homelessness, whether in Housing First programs or in the treatment- or sobriety-required supportive housing units. Research finds that for many, placement in housing is associated with reduced use of acute hospital, shelter, and justice services. Indeed, for some populations, such as those with severe mental disorders, frequent jail users, and the aging, the reduced service use fully offsets the cost of the housing—a win for taxpayers and a win for our neighbors, who could now be called *formerly* chronically homeless.

With this new evidence in hand, the Bush administration made it a federal goal to "end chronic homelessness" in its 2003 budget and directed the Department of Housing and Urban Development (HUD) to prioritize new funding for more supported housing. In the ensuing decade, the number of permanent supportive housing units has grown dramatically, from just over 150,000 in 2003 to 300,000 in 2014 nationally. And the number of people who experience chronic homelessness on a given night has declined by half.

Crisis Homelessness

In 2009 as the dimensions of the economic crisis were being felt, President Obama and Congress passed emergency stimulus spending. Federal housing officials contemplated how they could use this opportunity to mitigate the impact of the economic crisis on homelessness. Innovators in homelessness at the time had been experimenting with promising models to address crisis homelessness, including programs in Los Angeles, Minneapolis, New York City, and Mercer County, New Jersey. The emerging model, dubbed Homelessness Prevention and Rapid Rehousing (HPRP), was enacted as a national demonstration program as part of the American Recovery and Reinvestment Act of 2009. Under the program and consistent with previous research, homelessness was presumed to primarily affect people experiencing a short-term social or economic crisis, and with temporary services (e.g., emergency cash assistance and housing supports) people could resolve their homelessness relatively quickly and perhaps avoid it entirely. Indeed, as a result of the program, nearly 1 million people were served between 2010 and 2012. Unlike most other economic indicators of the recession, homelessness did not increase, other than a relatively small increase in 2010 among suburban and rural families as the program was just getting under way.

The HPRP concept has now been established in federal law as part of the renewed McKinney-Vento Act. HUD has created a new program, the Emergency Solutions Grant program, to allocate rapid rehousing resources and has encouraged communities to prioritize rapid rehousing in their main homelessness assistance programs, including through the conversion of more costly transitional housing programs.

With these innovations in policy and practice and supported by evaluation research, the field now has two solutions—supported housing and rapid rehousing—for chronic homelessness and crisis homelessness, respectively. The new federal plan to end homelessness, Opening Doors, has affirmed this direction in policy and is guiding federal agency resources using these two jointly labeled Housing First approaches.

Congress and HUD Build National Data Capacity
to Track Progress

Beginning in 2000, Congress called for all communities in the United States to develop computerized systems for tracking the use of homeless services and outcomes. The rationale was that through better data, communities would be able to more effectively target their resources and identify strategies that worked (and those that didn't) and that federal policy could also be better informed by this new system of information. The data collection process became known as Homelessness Services Management Information Systems (HMIS) and is governed by explicit federal data standards and security guidelines. While some communities are not fully using the data capacity created by HMIS, and indeed in some places it is viewed more as a data collection burden than benefit, others are recognizing that the HMIS data can form the core of a smarter and more strategic effort to end homelessness.

President Obama and Congress Invest
to End Veteran Homelessness

Building on the success of the Bush administration's chronic homelessness initiatives, the Obama administration and Congress turned their attention to the problem of homelessness among veterans. In 2009, U.S. Department of Veterans Affairs (VA) secretary Eric Shinseki charged his agency with ending veteran homelessness by 2015 and, with congressional support, mounted a major expansion of housing and services targeting the problem.

The first major program expansion was to the HUD-VA Supported Housing (VASH) program. The program had been a relatively minor effort to that point, linking two federal agencies—HUD to administer the housing vouchers and VA medical centers to provide the case management. However, under the Obama administration, the program grew from just over 8,000 units in 2008 to over 70,000 today. This major expansion in housing enabled the VA to reach tens of thousands of veterans on the streets and move them into permanent housing. Implementation was not without its challenges, and some communities have proved better at doing the outreach and making timely placements than others. But the VA has mounted a technical assistance and training effort to assist medical centers in the practice of Housing First and in the timely placement of people into housing. Perhaps no other program has contributed so much to the decline in veteran homelessness during the Obama administration, from an estimated 85,000 people at a given point in time in January 2009 to about 49,000 people five years later.

To address the problem of *crisis homelessness* among veterans, the VA launched a parallel program to HUD's HPRP program called Supported Services to Veteran Families (SSVF). Like the HPRP that preceded it, the SSVF offers both preventive interventions to households on the brink of homelessness and rapid rehousing to those who find themselves homeless in shelters or on the streets. The program provides assistance with debt reduction, rent arrears, and utility shutoffs as well as relocation assistance to households that have to move, including first and last months' rent and security deposits. The program also provides up to nine months of rental assistance based on need.

Like the HPRP program, the SSVF program has been a success and has contributed to the decline in veteran homelessness. Evaluations show that 85% of the households assisted do not return to homelessness up to one year after they have exited the program. Because most of the veteran households who are assisted consist of single adults, mostly men (mirroring the dominant population of adult homelessness more generally), the program has offered an important opportunity to test whether this rapid rehousing intervention model can work with single adults as well as families. Indeed, the evaluations show that the program, while slightly less effective for singles than families, is still associated with better than 80% retention in housing up to 12 months after exiting the program.

By relying on evidence-based practices and pairing up the prevention and rapid rehousing resources for veterans who experience crisis homelessness, these expanded VA programs are making a

significant dent in veteran homelessness. While zero veteran homelessness at any given time may be impossible to sustain, these programs hold the promise of reducing homelessness among veterans
even more steeply in just the next couple of years. Access to these
critical resources could mean that no veteran should be homeless
for more than 30 days and that, indeed, we can end *every* veteran's
homelessness quickly and effectively.

On the Horizon: Taking Supported Housing to Scale

The successes resulting from changes to homelessness policy and
practice demonstrate that combining knowledge from research,
innovations from the field, insights from the people who use these
programs, and a data-driven policy environment can lead to public policy victories. Human lives can benefit, as can society, from
a better and smarter approach to programs and services. But more
remains to be done. Homelessness continues to persist, especially
among nonveterans, and in some communities has even grown, as
these programs remain discretionary and are not funded sufficiently
to take them to scale. Indeed, it remains a striking fact that nearly
half of the homeless adults in this country, about 250,000 persons on
a given night, are living *unsheltered* on the streets, in cars, in parks,
or in other places not meant for human habitation, facing daily
threats to their health and safety.

Future sessions of Congress and the new president in 2017 will
have the chance to make a major difference in the lives of the many
people who suffer from homelessness or who are fated to become
homeless in the face of stark housing affordability problems and the
periodic crises that beset very poor people in our society. But proven
successes have provided the framework for making further progress,
and urgent action is needed.

First, the federal government should redouble its efforts to
address chronic homelessness. Just as it has expanded vouchers and
housing supports for veterans, it should commit itself to expanding

subsidies for supported housing to nonveterans. Approximately 80,000 people experience chronic homelessness on a given day, and an expansion in the number of vouchers targeting them by 20,000 a year for five years could effectively solve that problem. A focus on the aging homeless population also holds the promise of offsetting the costs of housing by reducing end-of-life health care costs. Nearly 50% of the chronic homeless population is over age 50. A program targeting people ages 55 and over, whose life expectancy is a mere 64 years, could help reduce hospitalizations and nursing home placements and fully offset the cost of their housing.

An expansion of rapid rehousing opportunities could also help to end homelessness, if not avert it, for the 135,000 families who experience homelessness annually. If the HPRP is a guide, the average household used approximately $3,500 in rent or cash supports to resolve its homelessness. Thus, a program of approximately $550 million could help to end family homelessness for all homeless families each year, possibly doing so in 30 days or less, as has been called for in the reauthorized McKinney Vento Act (also known as the HEARTH Act, for "Homeless Emergency Assistance and Rapid Transition to Housing"). Indeed, a revamping of the whole approach to addressing crisis homelessness, including for single adults, could build on the experiences of the HPRP and the SSVF and provide all people who become homeless with urgent crisis interventions, including emergency cash and supports, as an alternative to the neglect of long and repeated stays in barracks-style emergency shelters.

One emerging opportunity for expanding rapid rehousing for the single adult homeless as well as some families comes from the behavioral health field and the promise of newly expanded Medicaid eligibility. Under the Medicaid expansion of the Affordable Care Act, nearly all single adults who experience homelessness should now be eligible for Medicaid, at least in the states that adopt the expansion. Given that many of the single adults who experience crisis homelessness are also experiencing behavioral health issues, be they mental disorders or substance use disorders, and that many are also recently leaving institutions such as detoxification centers, inpatient psychiatric care, or jails, they may benefit from a Medicaid-funded behavioral health intervention known as Critical Time Intervention (CTI). CTI was established as a program to effectively transition people with behavioral health problems out of institutions and back to the community so they do not end up being readmitted to hospitals or detox programs or return to jails or homelessness. With many of the adults experiencing crisis homelessness now eligible for Medicaid and with CTI an eligible service for reimbursement (as long as states include it in their Medicaid plans), a great number of the single adults who experience homelessness may be able to get the social and health supports they need to both avoid homelessness and access stable housing either with their families or on their own. This could prove to completely change the way crisis homelessness is addressed, bringing to nonveterans some of the rapid rehousing support services currently provided to veterans.

Finally, continuing expansion of funds targeting homeless veterans could effectively end veteran homelessness for every homeless veteran in 30 days or less, with only modest further investments. It is likely that 10,000–20,000 additional VASH vouchers and a total of $500 million in SSVF annually could sufficiently meet the demands of both those veterans who are homeless today and those who are at risk in the future.

Housing Now!

The year 1990 marked the peak of homelessness activism, when several hundred thousand marchers gathered before the U.S. Capitol with the call "Housing Now!" to end the homelessness crisis. Initially progress was discouragingly slow, and street-level activism waned. But as research has improved and federal agencies and communities systematically turned their attention to housing solutions, we now know that people who previously suffered on the streets can be housed. Millions more can be, including poor families and individuals who experience crisis homelessness each year. All people can be quickly and effectively restored to dignity and safety if we can continue to draw from the best of evidence-based practices, organize our resources, convert our goodwill to political will, and convert our best of intentions into the best of practices.

Sources

Austin, E. L., Pollio, D. E., Holmes, S., Schumacher, J., White, B., Lukas, C. VanDeusen, & Kertesz, S. (2014). VA's expansion of supportive housing: Successes and challenges on the path toward Housing First. *Psychiatric Services, 65*(5), 641–47.

Blanch, A. K., Carling, P. J., & Ridgway, P. (1988). Normal housing with specialized supports: A psychiatric rehabilitation approach to living in the community. *Rehabilitation Psychology, 33*(1), 47–55.

Burt, M. R., Wilkins, C., & Mauch, D. (2011). *Medicaid and permanent supportive housing for chronically homeless individuals: Literature synthesis and environmental scan.* Washington, D.C.: HHS/ASPE.

Byrne, T., Culhane, D. P., Kane, V., Kuhn, J., & Treglia, D. (2014). *Predictors of homelessness following exit from the supportive services for veteran families program.*

Byrne, T., Fargo, J. D., Montgomery, A. E., Roberts, C. B., Culhane, D. P., & Kane, V. (In press). Screening for homelessness and risk in a national healthcare system: Monitoring housing stability through repeat screening and exploring profiles of risk. *Public Health Reports.*

Byrne, T., Kuhn, J., Culhane, D. P., Kane, S., & Kane, V. (2014). *Impact and performance of the Supportive Services for Veteran Families (SSVF) Program: Results from the FY 2013 program year.*

Byrne, T., Metraux, S., Moreno, M., Culhane, D. P., Toros, H., & Stevens, M. (2012). *Los Angeles County's Enterprise Linkages Project: An example of the use of integrated data systems in making data-driven policy and program decisions.*

Cortes, A., Rothschild, L., de la Cruz, R. J., Henry, M., Solari, C., Khadduri, J., & Culhane, D. P. (2012). *2011 Annual Homeless Assessment Report to Congress.*

Culhane, D. P., Dejowski, E. F., Ibanez, J., Needham, E., & Macchia, I. (1994). Public shelter admission rates in Philadelphia and New York City: The implications of turnover for sheltered population counts. *Housing Policy Debate, 5*(2), 107–40.

Culhane, D. P., & Metraux, S. (1999). One-year rates of public shelter utilization by race/ethnicity, age, sex and poverty status for New York City

(1990 and 1995) and Philadelphia (1995). *Population Research and Policy Review, 18*(3), 219–36.

———. (2008). Rearranging the deck chairs or reallocating the lifeboats? Homelessness assistance and its alternatives. *Journal of the American Planning Association, 74*(1), 111–21.

Culhane, D. P., Metraux, S., & Hadley, T. R. (2002a). The impact of supportive housing for homeless people with severe mental illness on the utilization of the public health, corrections, and emergency shelter systems: The New York-New York initiative. *Housing Policy Debate, 13*(1), 107–63.

———. 2002b. Public service reductions associated with placement of homeless persons with severe mental illness in supportive housing. *Housing Policy Debate, 13*(1), 107–63.

Gold, A. (1989). Thousands march on Washington in protest against homelessness. *New York Times*, October 8.

Henry, M., Cortes, A., Shivji, A., Buck, K., Khadduri, J., & Culhane, D. P. (2014). *The 2014 Annual Homelessness Assessment Report (AHAR) to Congress: Part 1; Point in time counts.*

Herman, D. B., Conover, S., Gorroochurn, P., Hinterland, K., Hoepner, L., & Susser, E. S. (2011). Randomized trial of critical time intervention to prevent homelessness after hospital discharge. *Psychiatric Services, 62*(7), 713–19.

Kuhn, R., & Culhane, D. P. (1998). Applying cluster analysis to test a typology of homelessness by pattern of shelter utilization: Results from the analysis of administrative data. *American Journal of Community Psychology, 26*(2), 207–32.

Larimer, M. E., Malone, D. K., Garner, M. D., Atkins, D. C., Burlingham, B., Lonczak, H. S., & Marlatt, A. (2009). Health care and public service use and costs before and after provision of housing for chronically homeless persons with severe alcohol problems. *JAMA, 301*(13), 1349–57.

Link, B. G., Susser, E., Stueve, A., Phelan, J., Moore, R. E., & Struening, E. (1994). Lifetime and five-year prevalence of homelessness in the United States. *American Journal of Public Health, 84*(12), 1907–12.

Metraux, S. (2002). *Taking different ways home: The intersection of mental illness, homelessness and housing in New York City.*

Montgomery, A. E. (2014). *Research brief: Using a universal screener to identify veterans experiencing housing instability.* Philadelphia: National Center on Homelessness Among Veterans.

Montgomery, A. E., Metraux, S., & Culhane, D. P. (2013a). *Ending veteran homelessness: Why HUD programs matter.*

———. (2013b). Rethinking homelessness prevention among persons with serious mental illness. *Social Issues and Policy Review, 7*(1), 58–82.

National Alliance to End Homelessness. (2014). *Rapid rehousing: A history and core components.*

Nelson, G., Aubry, T., & Lafrance, A. (2007). A review of the literature on the effectiveness of housing and support, assertive community treatment, and intensive case management interventions for persons with mental illness who have been homeless. *American Journal of Orthopsychiatry, 77*(3), 350–61.

Office of the President of the United States of America. (2002). *Budget of the U.S. government, fiscal year 2003.* Washington, DC: U.S. Government Printing Office.

O'Flaherty, B., & Goodman, S. (2012). *Does homelessness prevention work? Evidence from New York City's HomeBase Program.*

Poulin, S., Metraux, S., & Culhane, D. P. (2008). The history and future of Homeless Management Information Systems. In R. H. McNamara (Ed.), *Homelessness in America*, pp. 171–79. Westport, CT: Praeger.

Rog, D. J., Marshall, T., Dougherty, R. H., George, P., Daniels, A. S., Ghose, S. S., & Delphin-Rittmon, M. E. (2014). Permanent supportive housing: Assessing the evidence. *Psychiatric Services, 65*(3), 287–94.

Tabol, C., Drebing, C., & Rosenheck, R. (2010). Studies of "supported" and "supportive" housing: A comprehensive review of model descriptions and measurement. *Evaluation and Program Planning, 33*(4), 446–56.

Tsemberis, S., & Asmussen, S. (1999). From streets to homes: An innovative approach to supported housing for homeless adults with psychiatric disabilities. *Journal of Community Psychology, 27*(2), 225–41.

U.S. Department of Housing and Urban Development. (2010). *HPRP: Strategies for achieving performance and spending goals.*

U.S. Department of Veterans Affairs. (2009). *Secretary Shinseki details plan to end homelessness for veterans.*

U.S. Interagency Council on Homelessness. (2010). *Opening doors: Federal strategic plan to prevent and end homelessness.*

CHAPTER 2

Mass Incarceration

What's at Stake and What to Do

Malitta Engstrom, Alexandra Wimberly, and Nancy Franke

Mass incarceration in the United States has resulted in the largest national prison population of any country in the world and is one of the gravest social concerns of our time. Described by the *New York Times* as a destructive "40-year experiment" (New York Times Editorial Board, 2014), its profound human and economic costs extend far beyond the more than $80 billion spent annually on federal, state, and local corrections in the United States; the additional $58 billion spent on judicial and legal expenses; and the $126 billion spent on policing services (Kyckelhahn, 2015). With more than 2.2 million adults incarcerated, more than 4.7 million adults on probation or parole (Kaeble, Glaze, Tsoutis, & Minton, 2015), and disproportionate impact on people who are African American, Hispanic/Latino, experiencing mental health and substance use problems, and affected by poverty and limited education (Alexander, 2010; Carson, 2014, 2015; Engstrom, 2008; Gottschalk, 2015; James & Glaze, 2006; Karberg & James, 2005; Mauer & King, 2007; Mumola & Karberg, 2006; National Research Council, 2014; Prins, 2014; Schirmer, Nellis, & Mauer, 2009; Teplin, 1990, 1994; Teplin, Abram, & McClelland, 1996;

Torrey et al., 2014), the social costs are staggering. They include per-petuation of profound inequality, loss of liberty, and suffering at indi-vidual, family, and community levels in ways that are at odds with notions of the United States as a just society.

These economic and social costs have not yielded proportionate reductions in crime. In fact, as noted by the National Research Coun-cil (2014), crime rates rose and fell twice in the last four decades, despite the steady climb in incarceration. Using state-level data, the Brennan Center for Justice (Roeder, Eisen, & Bowling, 2015) finds that since the 1990s, greater incarceration has had essentially no effect on violent crime declines, and since 2000, there has been virtually no effect (0–1%) on property crime declines, with recent declines being partially attributed to alcohol use reduction, income growth and other economic factors such as inflation and consumer confidence, and the implementation of a data-driven approach to policing called CompStat. It should be noted that CompStat is not without limitations and critiques, including pressures in some police departments to show reductions in crime that may not be accurate. The Brennan Center analyses attempted to address this issue by drawing on data from numerous years and cities.

Oft-cited reasons for the extraordinary climb in incarceration include multiple changes in sentencing policies and practices. Most notable are increased risk of incarceration with arrest, lengthy man-datory minimum sentences that limit judicial discretion in sentenc-ing (including "three strikes and you're out" legislation that yields sentences of 25 years or more), limits on early release from incar-ceration, increased prison admissions for parole violations, and the context of the war on drugs, which involves a combination of height-ened policing and sentencing practices (Engstrom, 2008; National Research Council, 2014; New York Times Editorial Board, 2014). With tougher sentencing laws, prosecutors gained greater power in criminal charging decisions, which has led to greater use of plea bargaining. As described by Jed Rakoff (2014), a U.S. district judge, the proportion of federal cases going to trial dropped from 19% in 1980 to less than 6% in 2000 and to less than 3% in 2010. In plea bargaining, defendants are often pressured to enter a guilty plea or face more serious charges by prosecutors at trial—charges that are accompanied by tough mandatory sentences (Devers, 2011). The daunting risks of going to trial, even if a person is innocent, often prompt taking a plea bargain.

Political scientist Marie Gottschalk (2015) notes additional contributing factors, including increased income inequality, criminalization of poverty and immigration policy, erosion of social services, and larger economic and political forces that perpetuate mass incarceration and impede its recession. An implication of these disturbing trends in the United States is powerfully represented in a frequently quoted statement by Patrick Leahy (2013), U.S. senator from Vermont: "it is better to be rich and guilty than poor and innocent." An example of the skewed nature of the justice system toward people with financial means is the bail system. Many people with low risk, including people who are innocent, spend long periods in jail before their cases are heard because they don't have the financial means to pay for bail. This is especially troubling considering that approximately 60% of the U.S. jail population has not been convicted of pending charges (Bureau of Justice Statistics, 2015; Minton & Golinelli, 2014; Neal, 2012) and that such detention can have serious, long-lasting effects, as illuminated by the recent suicide and experiences of Kalief Browder, age 22 (Gonnerman, 2014, 2015; Schwirtz & Winerip, 2015). Beginning at age 16, he was held without sentencing for three years after primarily being accused of theft of a backpack and its contents. The charges were ultimately dropped, but not before he endured physical abuse by staff and other people incarcerated at Rikers Island and two years of solitary confinement.

After many years of limited attention and action, we are seeing broad recognition among liberal and conservative policy makers and advocates that mass incarceration must be addressed (Epperson & Pettus-Davis, 2015; New York Times Editorial Board, 2014; Stiglitz, 2015). Numerous municipalities across the country are enacting innovative policies and programs to reduce incarceration, and citizens are demanding criminal justice reform. As paths to change are considered, it will be important to ensure that clear attention is paid to what's at stake and what can be done to address mass incarceration, including recognition of the need for evidence-supported, multifaceted strategies.

Trends in Incarceration in the United States:
What's at Stake

It is generally recognized that unprecedented growth in incarceration in the United States began about four decades ago, due to policies and practices initially instituted in response to high rates of crime. As summarized by the American Civil Liberties Union (n.d.), the number of people in prison in the United States has grown by 700% since 1970, and despite having just under 5% of the global population, the United States has more than 20% of the world's imprisoned population (Lee, 2015). The Bureau of Justice Statistics reports that at the end of the year in 2014, there were 1,561,500 adults incarcerated in state and federal institutions (Carson, 2015). An additional 744,600 adults were incarcerated in local jails (Kaeble et al., 2015). These combined numbers translate into a rate of incarceration of 900 people out of every 100,000 U.S. adults, consistently among the highest rates in the world. Further, 1 in 36 adults in the United States was incarcerated, on probation, or on parole in 2014 (Kaeble et al., 2015). As Bryan Stevenson (2014) of the Equal Justice Initiative notes, between 1990 and 2005, a new prison was built every 10 days in the United States.

While men comprise the majority of adults incarcerated in prisons or local jails (approximately 92.7%), the number of incarcerated women has grown more quickly than that of men in recent years (Glaze & Kaeble, 2014; Minton & Zeng, 2015). Of particular note, there was a 3.2% reduction in the number of men incarcerated in local jails at midyear between 2010 and 2014; however, the number of women incarcerated in local jails grew by 18.1% during this time (Minton & Zeng, 2015). Additionally, when considering all people involved in the adult correctional system, including people who are on probation and parole, we see a higher percentage of women (approximately 18%; Glaze & Kaeble, 2014).

There are deeply disturbing disparities in rates of incarceration by race and ethnicity. African American adults comprise approximately 13% of the U.S. population over age 18; however, approximately 37% of men in prison and 21% of women in prison are African American (Carson, 2015; U.S. Census Bureau, 2014). A 2007 report from the Sentencing Project (Mauer & King, 2007) finds that the rates of incarceration among people who are African American or Hispanic/Latino are 5.6 and 1.8 times the rate among people who are White, respectively, and that there is considerable variation in these ratios by state. Harsh penalties related to immigration have created one of the fastest-growing populations affected by mass incarceration. Immigration-related charges made up over half of federal prosecutions in 2013 (Gottschalk, 2015). Between 2000 and 2010, there was an increase of nearly 60% in the number of people in state and federal prison who were Hispanic/Latino (Guerino, Harrison, & Sabol, 2012; Kilgore, 2014).

Intersections between gender, age, education, race, and ethnicity have resulted in extraordinary risk of incarceration among young African American men, particularly African American men with limited education. As described by the National Research Council (2014), 20% of African American men who haven't attended college have been incarcerated in state or federal prison at some point. This number jumps to 68% among African American men who did not complete high school. Between 1972 and 2010, there was a negligible increase in the rates of incarceration among men ages 20–39 with some college experience; however, the increases among men with no college and less than high school education were dramatic, especially among the latter group.

At every turn, we see that mass incarceration builds upon and exacerbates profound social inequality. This picture becomes even starker when considering the effects of incarceration on families. According to a revised 2008 Bureau of Justice Statistics report (Glaze & Maruschak, 2010), more than half of the people in state (52%) and federal (63%) prisons in the middle of 2007 were parents of children under age 18. At that time, it was estimated that their children comprised 2.3% of children in the United States and that approximately half of the children were quite young (9 years old or younger). African American and Hispanic/Latino children were 7.5 and 2.5 times, respectively, more likely than White children to be in this group, respectively. And this group didn't include the many children with a parent in local jails. A 2009 report from the Sentencing Project estimated that 1 in 15 African American children, 1 in 42 Hispanic/ Latino children, and 1 in 111 White children have a parent who is incarcerated (Schirmer, Nellis, & Mauer, 2009).

While resilience and functioning well in the face of adversity shouldn't be overlooked (Poehlmann & Eddy, 2013), having an incarcerated parent is associated with numerous challenges for children. The challenges can include behavioral and emotional problems, relational disruptions within the family, and often co-occurring risks associated with poverty, problematic substance use among parents, and numerous transitions in caregiving arrangements and schools (Engstrom, 2008). Relatedly, these challenges can affect the caregivers of children with incarcerated parents, who often provide critical material and emotional support not just for the children but also for the parents who are incarcerated (Engstrom, 2008).

The starkness of mass incarceration's intersections with social disadvantage and inequality is furthered by the disproportionate representation of people with mental illness, substance use problems, and histories of victimization who are involved in the U.S. criminal justice system (Harlow, 1999; James & Glaze, 2006; National Research Council, 2014; Teplin, 1990, 1994; Teplin, Abram, & McClelland, 1996; Winham, Engstrom, Golder, Renn, Higgins, & Logan, 2015). Nicholas Turner (2015) of the Vera Institute argues "that jails have become the provider of last resort for people with mental health issues" and that it is common for this group to be charged with nonviolent acts, to be unable to pay small bail amounts, and then to experience conditions that worsen their mental health, including abuse, inadequate health care, and excessive solitary confinement. A 2013 *Wall Street Journal* article (Fields & Phillips, 2013) noted that the three largest county jail systems in the United States (Cook County, Los Angeles County, and New York City) are also the country's largest mental health treatment facilities. Within these jails, 11,000 people received mental health treatment each day (of an approximate total population of 41,500 people in 2013); however, there are large numbers of people with mental health and substance use problems who do not receive treatment while incarcerated (James & Glaze, 2006; Teplin, Abram, & McClelland, 1997) and many whose lack of adequate treatment in the community is related to heightened risk of criminal justice system involvement (Evans, Li, Pierce, & Hser, 2013; Garnick et al., 2014; Kissin, Tang, Campbell, Claus, & Orwin, 2014; Van Dorn, Desmarais, Petrila, Haynes, & Singh, 2013). Especially given the context of the war on drugs and the disproportionate representation of people with substance use problems who are incarcerated (68% of people in local jails and approximately half of people in state [53.4%] and federal [45.5%] prisons are estimated to meet diagnostic criteria for a substance use disorder); (Karberg & James, 2005; Mumola & Karberg, 2006), it is stunning that the majority of people with need do not receive treatment while incarcerated, upon community return, or while on probation or parole (Belenko & Peugh, 2005; Karberg & James, 2005; Mumola & Karberg, 2006; Taxman, Perdoni, & Harrison, 2007).

And yet, as disturbing as all this is, the enduring consequences of incarceration exacerbate it further. As described by Marie Gottschalk (2015), millions of people are sentenced to "civil death" related to their incarceration. These effects involve ineligibility for public housing, student loans, food stamps, and numerous professional licenses, as well as restrictions on voting eligibility. In addition to these formal exclusions, a criminal record limits employment prospects and opportunities to rebuild one's life, support oneself and one's family, and avoid rearrest and reincarceration.

Ending Mass Incarceration: What to Do

Mass incarceration results from the intersection of multiple phenomena, including policing practices, sentencing policies, responses to substance use and mental illness, inadequate educational and vocational opportunities, and economic and political influences. Effective approaches will require multifaceted solutions informed by evidence and evaluated upon implementation to examine intended and unintended outcomes. We highlight several key strategies here.

Guiding Principles, Evaluation, and Changing Course When Indicated. The National Research Council (2014) asserts that while considering responsibility for one's actions and addressing crime, a well-informed approach should involve recognition of the harshness of imprisonment that extends to individuals, families, communities, and society and should take into account four principles: (1) *proportionality* between sentences and seriousness of the illegal activity; (2) *parsimony* so that sentences do not extend longer than needed; (3) *citizenship* so that effects of incarceration do not violate rights of citizens in lasting ways; and (4) *social justice* so that the use of incarceration supports the aims of a just, equitable society. We agree with these assertions and would add that policies and practices drawing upon these principles should be rigorously evaluated by nonpartisan parties to assess intended and unintended effects. The current context of mass incarceration makes it necessary to state an obvious, overlooked consideration: failed policies and practices should not continue to be funded, especially when they have dire consequences for individuals, families, communities, and society.

Sentencing. Sentencing reform efforts are developing to decrease sentence lengths and time served. For example, California recently passed Proposition 47, changing six nonviolent offenses from felonies to misdemeanors in the absence of prior violent convictions, which is projected to reduce the number of people incarcerated and the length of sentences. In 2012, California passed Proposition 36, providing opportunities for people with nonviolent, nonserious "third strike" convictions to be resentenced. A 2015 *New York Times* article (Eckholm, 2015) reported that over an 18-month period in California, there was a 4.7% reincarceration rate (typically for burglary or drug-related charges) among people released after prior life sentences, in comparison to a general rate of 45%. While such efforts reflect important steps toward addressing mass incarceration, numerous people have raised the importance of sentencing reform for more serious convictions. As described by Marc Mauer and David Cole (2015), "We could cut sentences for violent crimes by half in most instances without significantly undermining deterrence or increasing the threat of repeat offending." In addition to reviewing sentences according to the criteria above, it is critically important that the backlog within the courts be addressed immediately to ensure that the right to a speedy trial can be upheld.

Executive clemency. Currently, executive clemency (when a president or state governor grants leniency or a pardon) is parsimoniously given, a marked shift from the first half of this century (Gottschalk, 2015). President Barack Obama had a limited record of such action but may be making a shift as his presidency concludes (Sink, 2015; Shear, 2016)—he recently commuted drug-related sentences of 61 people, which, as of March 30, 2016, was reported to bring the total to 248 people who had their sentences commuted by him (Shear, 2016). While there is variation across states, governors rarely exercise this right.

Analysis of policy effects related to race, ethnicity, and gender. All policies related to incarceration should include what the Sentencing Project (Mauer & King, 2007) calls a "Racial Impact Statement" that would analyze potential race- and ethnicity-related effects prior to implementation. We would add that such pre-implementation analysis should include consideration of effects by gender and be followed by post-implementation analyses that consider effects by race, ethnicity, and gender.

Drug law reform. As federal and state governments have identified criminal justice policies and practices that don't work, changes have been initiated. For example, in New York, the disbandment of the Rockefeller Drug Laws (named for Governor Nelson Rockefeller, who advocated for the 1973 laws that are often considered the nation's most severe, with mandatory sentences of 15 years to life for the sale of two ounces or possession of four ounces of several drugs, including cocaine, heroin, and marijuana) has resulted in more people going to treatment rather than prison (Parsons, 2015). Multiple states have introduced bills to reduce penalties for various drug charges and provide alternatives to incarceration. Particularly given the high rates of victimization, problematic substance use, and mental health concerns among people who are involved with the criminal justice system (Harlow, 1999; James & Glaze, 2006; National Research Council, 2014; Teplin, 1990, 1994; Teplin, Abram, & McClelland, 1996; Winham et al., 2015), it is imperative to consider alternatives to incarceration that provide pathways to treatment and services and reduce the use of incarceration to address these underlying issues.

Alternatives to incarceration. A range of alternatives to incarceration must be further developed, researched, and, when shown to have positive effects, widely employed. While not without critiques, adult drug courts, which involve coordination among substance use treatment, social services, and criminal justice procedures and oversight, have been associated with reduced substance use and reinvolvement with the criminal justice system when compared to other conditions (Mitchell, Wilson, Eggers, & MacKenzie, 2012). Similar to drug courts, mental health courts refer people experiencing mental illness to court-monitored treatment rather than incarceration. Multisite research finds that participants in mental health courts have fewer arrests per year and days of incarceration than people in the usual treatment group (Steadman, Redlich, Callahan, Robbins, & Vesselinov, 2011).

Incentivize reform. Approximately $4 billion is provided by the federal government to cities and states to support criminal justice activities; however, current funding structures incentivize arrests and seizures. Instead, the federal government could financially reward states and cities for implementing approaches that decrease incarceration while supporting public safety (Chettiar, 2014; Fortier & Chettiar, 2014).

Evidence-guided emphasis on community reentry. Incarceration disrupts life in just about every imaginable way, often making the return to the community a nearly insurmountable challenge, particularly when combined with the effects of a criminal record on access to housing, employment, and educational resources. The stigma attached to having a felony record lasts a lifetime, as do some of the approximately "50,000 legally mandated collateral consequences" described by Lorelei Laird in a 2013 article in the *American Bar Association Journal*. With an estimated 93% of all people who are in prison returning home at some point (Petersilia, 2003), it is necessary to address community reentry from the outset of incarceration. Halden, a maximum security prison in Norway, exemplifies this approach, as described in a 2015 article in the *New York Times* (Benko, 2015). Its primary orientation is to prepare people to return to the community following incarceration. There are numerous practices and structures within the prison to support this aim; however, of particular note, preparation for community return involves steps to ensure housing, employment, and social support for each person *prior to leaving* the prison. Research conducted in the United States underscores the importance of housing, the ability to meet one's basic needs, access to health care, and attention to substance use issues as important factors in the risk for rearrest (Freudenberg, Daniels, Crum, Perkins, & Richie, 2005; Mallik-Kane & Visher, 2008; Luther, Reichert, Holloway, Roth, & Aalsma, 2011); however, evaluations of comprehensive community-based reentry programs that address these needs have found mixed results, with some studies finding positive effects on reinvolvement with the criminal justice system and substance use and others finding negative or no effects (Grommon, Davidson, & Bynum, 2013). It is critically important that the United States prioritize (1) research regarding community reentry programs, (2) identification of effective approaches, and (3) uptake of evidence-supported programs.

Family-focused services. Incarcerating individuals has ripple effects through families, social networks, and, often, communities. A growing body of research suggests that addressing parenting and connecting incarcerated parents with their children is associated with positive gains, including reduced involvement with the criminal justice system; however, such services have limited availability, and when they do exist, they rarely incorporate children's caregivers (for discussion, see Engstrom, 2008). Involving supportive significant others and children's caregivers holds tremendous untapped potential to yield multidimensional positive outcomes, including improved relational and emotional experiences for families and reduced risk of reincarceration for individuals. Research and program development in this area are critical to realizing this untapped potential. Further, it is critical to widely distribute resources that can assist families who are affected by incarceration. One such resource is the Sesame Street tool kit "Little Children, Big Challenges: Incarceration," which provides child-friendly tools for understanding incarceration, coping with its effects, and maintaining family connections. However, this tool kit has also drawn critiques for receiving fiscal support from the philanthropic division of BAE Systems, a Department of Defense contractor that relies on labor by people incarcerated at for-profit institutions (Trotter, 2013).

Substance use treatment. There are significant shortfalls in access to evidence-supported substance use treatment in the United States. Ensuring access to a wide range of evidence-supported psychosocial and pharmacological treatments for problematic substance use, including those that also address mental health and trauma, in the context of society at large and in the context of incarceration and community reentry is a promising strategy to reduce incarceration. A key element in this strategy involves the need for the United States to consistently move its response to substance use from a moral, criminal perspective to a public health perspective that recognizes the complexity of factors associated with substance use and substance use-related problems and draws upon science to support the health and well-being of individuals, families, communities, and society (Miller, Forcehimes, & Zweben, 2011).

A growing body of research suggests that substance use treatment in correctional facilities, especially when followed by community-based treatment during reentry, can yield gains (Belenko, Hiller, & Hamilton, 2013; Chandler, Fletcher, & Volkow, 2009; Grommon et al., 2013; National Institute on Drug Abuse, 2007; Taxman, 2009); however, ongoing challenges involve ensuring access to treatment within correctional facilities, connecting people to substance use treatment upon community return, and supporting ongoing engagement with substance use treatment in the community (Belenko & Peugh, 2005; Belenko, et al., 2013; Chandler et al., 2009; Grommon et al., 2013; Karberg & James, 2005; Mumola & Karberg, 2006; Taxman, 2009; Taxman et al., 2007). Emerging research is showing promise of medications, such as methadone, buprenorphine, and naltrexone, to reduce substance use upon community return (Belenko et al., 2013; Chandler et al., 2009; National Institute on Drug Abuse, 2007; Taxman, 2009). For example, for people who experience challenges with opioids (e.g., prescription pain medications and heroin), Vivitrol, which is extended-release naltrexone in a monthly injection, has been shown to reduce return to opioid use among men exiting jail (Lee et al., 2015). The Supervision Motivation Accountable Responsibility and Treatment program in Kentucky is an example of one probation service that provides Vivitrol through a partner clinic (Associated Press, 2015).

Mental health treatment. Inadequate community-based resources and stigma regarding mental health issues and treatment often conspire to keep people with mental illness from receiving necessary supports. This conspiring has been especially problematic in the wake of deinstitutionalization, which began in 1955 and involves transferring people out of state psychiatric hospitals and dramatically reducing the capacity of these hospitals. A report from the Treatment Advocacy Center (Torrey et al., 2014) estimates that jails and prisons house 10 times the number of people with serious mental illness than state psychiatric hospitals. A wide range of interventions for people with mental illness is required to curtail incarceration and its related costs, which exceed those of community treatment (e.g., American Psychiatric Association, 2001). Needed interventions include access to evidence-supported mental health and integrated substance use treatment, housing, vocational resources, and social services to support positive functioning and quality of life for people experiencing mental illness, their families, and their communities (Corrigan, 2016; Lamberti, Weisman, & Faden, 2004). Early steps to reduce the risk of initial and continued criminal justice system involvement, including improved police response to people with mental illness, are also needed. One such model involves crisis intervention teams that consist of police officers trained to respond to people experiencing mental health crises and collaborating medical centers that provide emergency mental health services (Corrigan, 2016; Watson & Fulambarker, 2012). Though there have been mixed findings, use of such teams carries the potential to decrease arrests and mental health symptoms and to increase linkages to mental health services among people they serve (Arey, Wilder, Normore, Iannazzo, & Javidi, 2016; Taheri, 2016; Watson & Fulambarker, 2012). Research also supports the potential of jail diversion programs among people experiencing co-occurring mental illness and substance use problems to reduce jail time and improve treatment participation (Steadman & Naples, 2005). If diversion isn't possible, adequate mental health care, on par with needed medical care, is necessary for people with mental illness who are incarcerated, as is reentry planning to ensure linkages to community-based treatment and services (Corrigan, 2016). The Affordable Care Act offers funding opportunities for states that opt in to Medicaid expansion to provide mental health and substance use services for people upon community return.

Education. Education, including completing high school and college, buffers against the risk of incarceration (National Research Council, 2014). Based on factors noted by the American Civil Liberties Union (n.d.) that contribute to what has been called the "school-to-prison pipeline," it is critical that there be

(1) adequate funding and resources for public schools so that all students can thrive and remain in school;
(2) due process and proportionality in school discipline;
(3) examination and implementation of the most effective ways to ensure student safety, support relationships between students, teachers, and staff, and avoid police presence in schools (some may be surprised to learn of schools where police officers patrol hallways and

provide criminal consequences for nonviolent disruptive behavior);

(4) appropriate oversight of disciplinary alternative schools to ensure that students receive needed education that strengthens their opportunities upon completion; and

(5) within the juvenile justice system, appropriate legal representation, educational opportunities, and strategies to support positive trajectories for youth.

Grassroots efforts. Ongoing grassroots efforts will be important to ensure that current attention to mass incarceration is sustained and backed by multifaceted strategies to address the complex factors that fuel it. Many individuals and groups are advocating for greater equality and justice, improved immigration policy, and reductions in severe sentences and lasting consequences of incarceration. Grassroots advocacy can make a difference. For example, as described by the Sentencing Project (2015), collaborative efforts between Out for Justice and the Job Opportunities Task Force played significant roles in the enactment of Maryland's Second Chance Act of 2015. To learn more and to get involved in action to address mass incarceration, see the numerous resources and organizations listed at http://newjimcrow.com/take-action.

There is growing recognition that the magnitude of mass incarceration in the United States and its effects on individuals, families, communities, and society demand action. To be effective, such action will require attention to multifaceted strategies that address intersecting social concerns. Let us capitalize on the current calls for change to ensure that evidence-supported, multifaceted action regarding mass incarceration remains a national priority and fulfills the promise of the United States as a just society.

Sources

Alexander, M. (2010). *The new Jim Crow: Mass incarceration in the age of colorblindness.* New York, NY: New York University Press.

American Civil Liberties Union. (n.d.). Combating mass incarceration—the facts. Retrieved from https://www.aclu.org/infographic-combating-mass-incarceration-facts?redirect=combating-mass-incarceration-facts-0.

————. (n.d.). What is the school-to-prison pipeline? Retrieved from https://www.aclu.org/fact-sheet/what-school-prison-pipeline.

American Psychiatric Association. (2001). Gold Award: Helping mentally ill people break the cycle of jail and homelessness—The Thresholds, State, County Collaborative Jail Linkage Project, Chicago. *Psychiatric Services, 52*(10), 1380–82.

Associated Press. (2015). Kentucky officials hope drugs can help drug addicts. *NewsOk.*

Arey, J. B., Wilder, A. H., Normore, A. H., Iannazzo, M. D., & Javidi, M. (2016). Crisis intervention teams: An evolution of leadership in community and policing. *Policing, 10*(2), 143–49.

Belenko, S., Hiller, M., & Hamilton, L. (2013). Treating substance use disorders in the criminal justice system. *Current Psychiatry Reports, 15*(11), 414.

Belenko, S., & Peugh, J. (2005). Estimating drug treatment needs among state prison inmates. *Drug and Alcohol Dependence, 77*(33), 269–81.

Benko, J. (2015). The radical humaneness of Norway's Halden Prison. *New York Times*, March 26.

Bureau of Justice Statistics. (1982). *Prisoners 1925–81* (NCJ 85861). Washington, DC: U.S. Department of Justice, Bureau of Justice Statistics.

————. (2015). The nation's jails held fewer inmates at midyear 2014 compared to their peak count in 2008. Press release. Washington, DC: U.S. Department of Justice, Bureau of Justice Statistics.

Carson, E. A. (2014). *Prisoners in 2013* (NCJ 247282). Washington, DC: U.S. Department of Justice, Office of Justice Programs, Bureau of Justice Statistics.

————. (2015). *Prisoners in 2014* (NCJ 248955). Washington, DC: U.S. Department of Justice, Office of Justice Programs, Bureau of Justice Statistics.

Chandler, R. K., Fletcher, B. W., & Volkow, N. D. (2009). Treating drug abuse and addiction in the criminal justice system: Improving public health and safety. *JAMA, 301*(2), 183–90.

Chettiar, I. (2014). Feds can help reform police, but watch out for unintended consequences. *Reuters.*

Clarke, M. (2013). Dramatic increase in percentage of criminal cases being plea bargained. *Prison Legal News.*

Corrigan, P. (2016). *Principles and practice of psychiatric rehabilitation: An empirical approach* (2nd ed.). New York: Guilford.

Devers, L. (2011). *Plea and charge bargaining: Research summary.* Washington, DC: Bureau of Justice Assistance, U.S. Department of Justice.

Eckholm, E. (2015). Out of prison, and staying out, after 3rd strike in California. *New York Times.*

Engstrom, M. (2008). Involving caregiving grandmothers in family interventions when mothers with substance use problems are incarcerated. *Family Process, 47,* 357–71.

Epperson, M., & Pettus-Davis, C. (2015). Reducing Illinois prison population is a marathon not a sprint. *Chicago Sun Times.*

Evans, E., Li, L., Pierce, J., & Hser, Y.-I. (2013). Explaining long-term outcomes among drug dependent mothers treated in women-only versus mixed-gender programs. *Journal of Substance Abuse Treatment, 45*(3), 293–301.

Fellner, J. (2006). Corrections quandary: Mental illness and prison rules. *Harvard. CR-CLL Review, 41,* 391–412.

Fields, G., & Phillips, E. E. (2013). The new asylums: Jails swell with mentally ill. *Wall Street Journal.*

Fortier, N., & Chettiar, I. (2014). *Success-oriented funding: Reforming federal criminal justice grants.* New York, NY: Brennan Center for Justice.

Freudenberg, N., Daniels, J., Crum, M., Perkins, T., & Richie, B. E. (2005). Coming home from jail: The social and health consequences of community reentry for women, male adolescents, and their families and communities. *American Journal of Public Health, 95*(10), 1725–36.

Garnick, D. W., Horgan, C. M., Acevedo, A., Lee, M. T., Panas, L., Ritter, G. A., . . . Wright, D. (2014). Criminal justice outcomes after engagement in outpatient substance abuse treatment. *Journal of Substance Abuse Treatment, 46*(3), 295–305.

Glaze, L. E., & Kaeble, D. (2014). *Correctional populations in the United States, 2013* (NCJ 248479). Washington, DC: U.S. Department of Justice, Office of Justice Programs, Bureau of Justice Statistics.

Glaze, L. E., & Maruschak, L. M. (2008, revised 2010). *Parents in prison and their minor children* (NCJ 222984). Washington, DC: U.S. Department of Justice, Office of Justice Programs, Bureau of Justice Statistics.

Gonnerman, J. (2014). Before the law. *New Yorker,* October 6.

———. (2015). Kalief Browder, 1993–2015. *New Yorker,* June 7.

Gottschalk, M. (2015). *Caught: The prison state and the lockdown of American politics.* Princeton, NJ: Princeton University Press.

Grommon, E., Davidson, W. S., & Bynum, T. S. (2013). A randomized trial of a multimodal community-based prisoner reentry program emphasizing substance abuse treatment. *Journal of Offender Rehabilitation, 52*(4), 287–309.

Guerino, P., Harrison, P. M., & Sabol, W. (2011, revised 2012). *Prisoners in 2010* (NCJ 236096). U.S. Department of Justice, Office of Justice Programs, Bureau of Justice Statistics.

Harlow, C. W. (1999). *Prior abuse reported by inmates and probationers* (NCJ 1782879). Washington, DC: U.S. Department of Justice, Office of Justice Programs, Bureau of Justice Statistics.

Human Rights Watch. (2013). *An offer you can't refuse: How US federal prosecutors force drug defendants to plead guilty.* New York, NY: Human Rights Watch.

James, D. J., & Glaze, L. E. (2006). *Mental health problems of prison and jail inmates* (NCJ 213600). Washington, DC: U.S. Department of Justice, Office of Justice Programs, Bureau of Justice Statistics.

Kaeble, D., Glaze, L., Tsoutis, A., & Minton, T. (2015, revised 2016). *Correctional populations in the United States, 2014* (NCJ 249513). Washington, DC: U.S. Department of Justice, Office of Justice Programs, Bureau of Justice Statistics.

Karberg, J. C., & James, D. J. (2005). *Substance dependence, abuse, and treatment of jail inmates, 2002* (NCJ 209588). Washington, DC: U.S. Department of Justice, Office of Justice Programs, Bureau of Justice Statistics.

Kearney, M. S., Harris, B. H., Jacome, E., & Parker, L. (2014). *Ten economic facts about crime and incarceration in the United States.* Washington, DC: Hamilton Project.

Kilgore, J. (2014). Prop 47, immigration reform and more: The contradictory road of "reforming" mass incarceration. *Truthout.*

Kissin, W. B., Tang, Z., Campbell, K. M., Claus, R. E., & Orwin, R. G. (2014). *Journal of Substance Abuse Treatment, 46*(3), 332–39.

Kyckelhahn, T. (2015). *Justice expenditure and employment extracts, 2012: Preliminary.* Bureau of Justice Statistics, http://www.bjs.gov/index.cfm?ty=pbdetail&iid=5239.

Laird, L. (2013). Ex-offenders face tens of thousands of legal restrictions, bias and limits on their rights. *American Bar Association Journal.*

Lamberti, J. S., Weisman, R., & Faden, D. I. (2004). Forensic assertive community treatment: Preventing incarceration of adults with severe mental illness. *Psychiatric Services, 55*(11), 1285–93.

Leahy, P. (2013, March 18). On the fiftieth anniversary of Gideon v. Wainwright and the introduction of the Gideon's Promise Act of 2013. Retrieved from

https://www.leahy.senate.gov/press/on-anniversary-of-historic-scotus
-decision-leahy-introduces-gideons-promise-act.

Lee, J. D., McDonald, R., Grossman, E., McNeely, J., Laska, E., Rotrosen, J., & Gourevitch, M. N. (2015). Opioid treatment at release from jail using extended-release naltrexone: A pilot proof of concept randomized effectiveness trial. *Addiction, 110*(6), 1008–14.

Lee, M. Y. H. (2015). Does the United States really have 5 percent of the world's population and one quarter of the world's prisoners? *Washington Post.*

Mallik-Kane, K., & Visher, C. A. (2008). *Health and prisoner reentry: How physical, mental, and substance abuse conditions shape the process of reintegration.* Washington, DC: Urban Institute.

Mauer, M., & Cole, D. (2015). How to lock up fewer people. *New York Times.*

Mauer, M., & King, R. S. (2007). *Uneven justice: State rates of incarceration by race and ethnicity.* Washington, DC: Sentencing Project.

Miller, W. R., Forcehimes, A. A., & Zweben, A. (2011). *Treating addiction: A guide for professionals.* New York, NY: Guilford Press.

Minton, T. D., & Golinelli, D. (2014). *Jail inmates at midyear 2013—Statistical tables (NCJ 245350).* Washington, DC: U.S. Department of Justice, Office of Justice Programs, Bureau of Justice Statistics.

Mitchell, O., Wilson, D. B., Eggers, A., & MacKenzie, D. L. (2012). Assessing the effectiveness of drug courts on recidivism: A meta-analytic review of traditional and non-traditional drug courts. *Journal of Criminal Justice, 40*(1), 60–71.

Mumola, C. J., & Karberg, J. C. (2006). *Drug use and dependence, state and federal prisoners, 2004* (NCJ 213530). Washington, DC: U.S. Department of Justice, Office of Justice Programs, Bureau of Justice Statistics.

National Institute on Drug Abuse. (2007). *Principles of drug abuse treatment for criminal justice populations* (NIH Publication No. 11-5316). Washington, DC: National Institutes of Health, National Institute on Drug Abuse.

National Research Council. (2014). *The growth of incarceration in the United States: Exploring causes and consequences.* Washington, DC: National Academies Press.

Neal, M. (2012). *Bail fail: Why the U.S. should end the practice of using money for bail.* Washington, DC: Justice Policy Institute.

New York Times Editorial Board. (2014). End mass incarceration now. *New York Times.*

Parsons, J. (2015). *End of an era? The impact of drug law reform in New York City.* New York, NY: Vera Institute.

Petersilia, J. (2003). *When prisoners come home: Parole and prisoner reentry.* New York, NY: Oxford University Press.

Poehlmann, J., & Eddy, J. M. (2013). Relationship processes and resilience in children with incarcerated parents. *Monographs of the Society for Research in Child Development, 78*(3), 1–6.

Prins, S. J. (2014). Prevalence of mental illnesses in U.S. state prisons: A systematic review. *Psychiatric Services, 65*(7), 862–72.

Rakoff, J. S. (2014). Why innocent people plead guilty. *New York Review of Books,* November 20.

Roeder, O., Eisen, L-B., & Bowling, J. (2015). *What caused the crime decline?* New York, NY: Brennan Center for Justice.

Sarteschi, C. M., Vaughn, M. G., & Kim, K. (2011). Assessing the effectiveness of mental health courts: A quantitative review. *Journal of Criminal Justice, 39*(1), 12–20.

Schirmer, S., Nellis, A., & Mauer, M. (2009). *Incarcerated parents and their children: Trends, 1991–2007.* Washington, DC: Sentencing Project.

Schwirtz, M., & Winerip, M. (2015). Kalief Browder, held at Rikers Island for 3 years without trial, commits suicide. *New York Times.*

The Sentencing Project. (2013). *Report of the Sentencing Project to the United Nations Human Rights Committee regarding racial disparities in the United States criminal justice system.* Washington, DC: Sentencing Project.

———. (2015, June 1). State advocacy update: Grassroots strategy to address mass incarceration. Retrieved from http://www.sentencingproject.org /news/state-advocacy-update-grassroots-strategy-to-address-mass -incarceration/.

Shear, M. D. (2016). Obama commutes sentences for 61 convicted of drug crimes. *New York Times.*

Sink, J. (2015). Obama commutes sentences for 22 convicted of federal drug crimes. *Bloomberg.*

Steadman, H. J., & Naples, M. (2005). Assessing the effectiveness of jail diversion programs for persons with serious mental illness and co-occurring substance use disorders. *Behavioral Sciences & the Law, 23*(2), 163–70.

Steadman, H. J., Redlich, A., Callahan, L., Robbins, P. C., & Vesselinov, R. (2011). Effect of mental health courts on arrests and jail days: A multisite study. *Archives of General Psychiatry, 68*(2), 167–72.

Stevenson, B. (2014). *Just mercy: A story of justice and redemption.* New York, NY: Spiegel & Grau.

Stiglitz, J. E. (2015). Foreword. In O. Roeder, L-B. Eisen, & Julia Bowling (Authors). *What caused the crime decline?* New York, NY: Brennan Center for Justice.

Taheri, S. A. (2016). Do crisis intervention teams reduce arrests and improve officer safety? A systematic review and meta-analysis. *Criminal Justice Policy Review, 27*(1), 76–96.

Taxman, F. S. (2009). Drug treatment for offenders: Evidence-based criminal justice and treatment practices. Testimony provided to the Subcommittee on Commerce, Justice, Science, and Related Agencies. Retrieved from https://www.gmuace.org/documents/presentations/2009/2009-presentations-drug-treatment-for-offenders.pdf.

Taxman, F. S., Perdoni, M. L., & Harrison, L. D. (2007). Drug treatment services for adult offenders: The state of the state. *Journal of Substance Abuse Treatment, 32*(3), 239–54.

Teller, J. L. S., Munetz, M. R., Gil, K. M., & Ritter, C. (2006). Crisis intervention team training for police officers responding to mental disturbance calls. *Crisis, 57*(2), 232–37.

Teplin, L. A. (1990). The prevalence of severe mental disorder among male urban jail detainees: Comparison with the Epidemiologic Catchment Area Program. *American Journal of Public Health, 80*(6), 663–69.

———. (1994). Psychiatric and substance abuse disorders among male urban jail detainees. *American Journal of Public Health, 84*(2), 290–93.

Teplin, L. A., Abram, K. M., & McClelland, G. M. (1996). Prevalence of psychiatric disorders among incarcerated women: I. Pretrial jail detainees. *Archives of General Psychiatry, 53*(6), 505–12.

———. (1997). Mentally disordered women in jail: Who receives services? *American Journal of Public Health, 87*(4), 604–9.

Torrey, E. F., Zdanowicz, M. T., Kennard, A. D., Lamb, H. R., Eslinger, D. F., Biasotti, M. C., & Fuller, D. A. (2014). *The treatment of persons with mental illness in prisons and jails: A state survey.* Arlington, VA: Treatment Advocacy Center.

Trotter, J. K. (2013). Why is a defense contractor paying for Sesame Street's parents-in-jail lesson? *The Wire.*

Turner, N. (2015). Stop placing the mentally ill in jails. *New York Times.*

U.S. Census Bureau. (2014). *Annual estimates of the resident population by sex, age, race, and Hispanic origin for the United States and States: April 1, 2010 to July 1, 2014.*

Van Dorn, R. A., Desmarais, S. L., Petrila, J., Haynes, D., & Singh, J. P. (2013). Effects of outpatient treatment on risk of arrest of adults with serious mental illness and associated costs. *Psychiatric Services, 64*, 856–62.

Watson, A. C., & Fulambarker, A. J. (2012). The Crisis Intervention Team model of police response to mental health crises: A primer for mental health practitioners. *Best Practices in Mental Health, 8*(2), 71.

Wexler, H. K., & Fletcher, B. W. (2007). National criminal justice drug abuse studies (CJ-DATS) overview. *Prison Journal, 87*(1), 9–24.

Wildeman, C. (2012). Mass incarceration. *Oxford Bibliographies.*

Winham, K. M., Engstrom, M., Golder, S., Renn, T., Higgins, G. E., & Logan, T. K. (2015). Childhood victimization, attachment, psychological distress, and substance use among women on probation and parole. *American Journal of Orthopsychiatry, 85*(2), 145–58.

CHAPTER 3

Social Workers or the
Social Work Bureaucracy?

Antonio Garcia and Christina Denard

Three infants were found dead in a deplorable vermin-infested home in Massachusetts. The mother, Erika Murray, reportedly mentally ill, was arraigned on charges of fetal death concealment and substantial injury to a child. In the same state, a five-year-old boy's disappearance went unnoticed for months even though the boy's family had been monitored by the agency for years. Three social workers from the Massachusetts Department of Children and Families were fired after an investigation revealed that they missed visits and failed in attempts to engage with the family. In Los Angeles, Isauro Aguirre admitted to law enforcement that he hit his girlfriend's son, Gabriel Fernandez, eight years of age, at least 10 times for lying and "being dirty" right before he was pronounced dead. Despite previous reports and statements by Gabriel alleging abuse, no further action to intervene on his behalf was taken by the Department of Children and Family Services.

These severe cases of maltreatment and death may lead many of us to question the judgment and skill set of social workers. They become easy targets of our concern and anger. In the process, the bureaucracy impeding social workers from doing their best to protect children often remains unquestioned, and people feel powerless to challenge it. Bureaucracies seem at times too large, too convoluted, or too powerful to ever change. Few may know of the practical changes that can be implemented or consider how political elections can impact the work conditions of social workers and subsequently the safety of children under their supervision.

While negligent social workers should be held accountable, we need to support the restructuring of organizations and the reallocation of funds to better support caseworkers so that children are properly protected. In this vein, our chapter draws attention to key problems of the social work bureaucracy and offers solutions, including those that can be voted for during election season.

The Social Work Bureaucracy

Social workers are employed in a bureaucratic system in which they are overworked, underpaid, and not adequately trained and lack supervision. They are asked to respond to an overwhelming number of cases that require a high level of attention, critical assessment, and timely and effective intervention services to prevent death, preserve families, and promote child safety and well-being.

In 2013, over 400,000 children were placed in foster care due to incidents of abuse and neglect (UDHHS, 2014). However, a significant amount of time, resources, and effort is allocated to cases that are investigated and yet unsubstantiated, leaving only limited time to respond to the cases that warrant close monitoring and attention. According to recent statistics, over 2 million reports of child abuse and neglect are accepted to be investigated, and of those cases approximately 700,000 are judged to involve victims of abuse and neglect (UDHHS, 2011). Caseworkers often report that they are under constant stress from negotiating the multiple demands of their job (Garcia et al., 2015). The sheer volume of Child Protective Services (CPS) reports and investigations, the number of youths in foster care who need to be looked after, and the piles of paperwork to track decision making would overwhelm many under the best of circumstances.

The Child Welfare League of America recommends that a caseworker should have to manage no more than 17 active families. The recommended limits are lower for some cases: 12 families for initial investigations of alleged child abuse and 15 children for foster care cases. However, the average caseload for child welfare workers often exceeds recommended levels, sometimes by double or more (Child Welfare League of America, 2001). According to Carla Damron, executive director of the National Association of Social Workers in South Carolina, making the wrong call on a possible abuse case is a result of high caseloads (Self, 2014). To make matters worse, caseworkers and supervisors are called upon to urgently respond to cases within a small window of time, leaving little time or motivation to think critically and thoughtfully in decision making (Buckley et al., 2014). Instead, under such pressure, they are likely to use mental shortcuts or schemas based on split-second appraisals to dictate the fate of a child's life (Fedoravicius et al., 2008).

The consequences of using shortcuts likely include lack of timely and thorough CPS investigations, lack of timely permanency, multiple placement moves, and lack of effective engagement with youths and families—all factors that contribute to many youths "falling through the cracks" or even worse, placing them among the more than 1,500 children nationally who meet their demise prematurely due to abuse and neglect, such as Gabriel. And sadly, about 80% of all fatalities are children younger than four years old (U.S. Department of Health and Human Services, 2011).

Managing too many cases may only partially explain why caseworkers are likely to burn out. A number of studies show that caseworkers are embedded in agencies that do not provide them adequate training in the conduct of culturally competent care or supervision and work day after day in stressful organizational climates that often increase staff turnover. Lack of autonomy due to stringent bureaucratic policies and procedures adds fuel to the fire (Bowen et al., 2009; Collins-Camargo et al., 2011). How can caseworkers be expected to effectively screen and investigate referrals and promote safety and well-being in a timely manner under such conditions?

Many of the youths who enter foster care face many challenges in other systems of care such as law enforcement, juvenile justice, schools, mental health, and homeless shelters. Yet caseworkers often report how difficult it is to communicate and collaborate with providers across other sectors of care. Lack of information and data sharing to evaluate and monitor outcomes only serves to sustain gaps in service delivery. As one case manager reports in a study conducted by us and our colleagues, "Having services are great, but if you can't take on either the amount of referrals or make it difficult for us to make these referrals and actually get [mental health] treatment for our clients, that could be a serious barrier" (Garcia et al., 2015). In addition to high caseloads, staff turnover, and lack of interagency collaboration, child welfare agencies are faced with negotiating budget crises and hiring freezes, recruiting and retaining qualified applicants for open positions, and implementing time-intensive best practices (Day & Peterson, 2008).

Implementation of evidence-based and promising practices to reduce risk of abuse and neglect is contingent upon many external factors, such as access to and interaction with external agencies and availability of information, data management, funding, trained staff, and technology, to name a few (Aarons et al., 2011). Preventing poor outcomes and eliminating child fatalities are virtually impossible unless structural and systemic barriers are addressed and caseworkers have the tools and resources at their disposal. This brings us back to the importance of recognizing that the caseworker is not solely to blame for child fatalities and poor child and family outcomes. Rather, we must also pay attention to the ways that context and larger sociostructural and bureaucratic systems dictate whether and how caseworkers are able to promote safety, permanency, and well-being and how systemic barriers shape and reinforce injustice and inequality. Doing so allows us to see how changes in the bureaucracy can help caseworkers be more effective in ensuring the safety of children.

Solutions

Connect children and families to effective services. While we have argued for more attention paid to structural and systemic barriers, we do not want to undermine the importance of caseworker practice behaviors. Having the tools is paramount, but caseworkers also need to be trained in and be aware of what services are effective in their respective communities and for the target population they are serving. Caseworkers must be able to appropriately screen and assess need and be connected to referral resources in the community for children to receive timely and effective services that will eliminate risk of abuse and neglect (Garcia et al., 2015).

Disseminate and implement effective strategies. Recognizing the importance of community resources, however, is not enough. We must work toward identifying, disseminating, and implementing the most effective policy and practice strategies. There are a number of polices that aim to prevent poor outcomes. The Adoptions and Safe Families Act of 1997 was enacted to promote permanency and prevent children from lingering in foster care. The Child Abuse Prevention and Treatment Act of 1974 provides federal funding for states to respond to and investigate allegations of child maltreatment and occurrences of child fatalities. The Indian Child Welfare Act of 1978 was passed into legislation to prevent children of Native American ancestry from losing familial and tribal connections. All of these polices if implemented as intended may play an instrumental role in promoting positive outcomes and preventing child fatalities. More accountability and court oversight are needed to ensure that cases adhere to federal policy, and then these policies can be evaluated to determine if they actually improve child outcomes.

Reallocate resources. Oftentimes funding may be available. It is just a matter of *how* it is allocated. Are resources being allocated in areas where they are direly needed? Redistribution of funding to hire more staff to manage high caseloads and dollars is all too often recommended. The buck should not stop there. To prevent child maltreatment and fatalities, we need to ensure that innovative and effective programs and services are available and reachable to children and families.

Training. Ongoing training for caseworkers and supervisors is needed to ensure that they are aware of effective practices strategies and know how to deliver them (or at least know others in the community who are trained to implement them). They also need training to monitor client progress over time and detect when a case warrants more intensive intervention. Attention to the individuals and populations who are served by child welfare agencies is also paramount.

Develop and implement effective decision-making tools. The overrepresentation of children of color in the foster care system is by and large a by-product of a series of injustices. They are more likely to be placed and remain in foster care for lengthier periods of time compared to their Caucasian counterparts. To make matters worse, research over the past 15 years shows that Latino/a and African American youths are less likely to access effective mental health services (Garcia et al., 2013). Evidence-informed case decision-making tools, services, and programs are needed to end the cycle of racial inequity. We should all work diligently to ensure that children, regardless of their racial/ethnic background, receive quality services and are not reported by the media as being among the many children who meet their untimely demise. Communication and interagency collaboration will likely promote effective decision making (Palinkas et al., 2014).

Prevention is needed. For those who talk dollars and cents, research shows that the total cost of new cases of fatal and nonfatal child maltreatment in the United States was approximately $124 billion in 2008. The estimated cost per victim of nonfatal child maltreatment was $210,012 in 2010 due to medical/health care costs, productivity losses, child welfare costs, criminal justice costs, and special education expenditures. For fatal cases, the figure rises to an astonishing $1,272,900 per death (Fang et al., 2012). Fiscally, we can and should allocate funds for preventive measures to save money in the long run.

Create job support. Caseworkers need support. If we have not convinced you otherwise, take a page from my (Antonio's) own personal experience as a caseworker. For four years, I investigated allegations of child maltreatment after receiving a master's degree in social work. I was educated, having completed a yearlong internship in a child welfare agency prior to gaining employment, and yet I was still utterly and completely overwhelmed—not with just the sheer volume of cases but also with the severity of needs that many of the families had. There were countless times when clients were put on long waiting lists to receive services and resources and countless times when children and families were left to their own devices. With training, I was able to critically rely on theory and evidence and amend them to client situations and contexts as needed. And yet, I felt as though I was literally putting Band-Aid solutions on seemingly impossible and intractable public health concerns—violence and trauma of all forms that one cannot and should not imagine, substance abuse, drug dealing, mental health problems, poverty, gang violence, and homelessness, to name a few. I came into the office one morning to learn that I had been assigned to investigate a case in which the mother had stabbed her three-year-old daughter 26 times. I never met this family before but quickly found out that not too long ago the case was closed, despite the fact that there was no evidence that the mother received treatment for bipolar disorder. Cases such as these and the realization that many of the kids and families I met were either Latino/a or African American motivated me to pursue a doctoral degree in social welfare to address the systemic barriers I encountered. Let's hope that we can cultivate child welfare agencies to support caseworkers for their sake and for the children and families who need to heal from a number of traumas and injustices.

How Can You Get Involved?

Many of the issues addressed here—training, job support, and budget crises—can be directly impacted by an increase in or reallocation of funds that child welfare agencies receive. That money matters is obvious, but you may think that helping agencies get more funding is out of your reach. It's not. Since child welfare agencies receive a combination of federal, state, and local government funds, there are ways that voters can have an impact.

Of the funds spent on child welfare services, the largest funding stream is from the Title IV-E provision in the Social Security Act. This provision provides funds to support children in foster care, provide assistance to children with special needs that are adopted or will be under guardianship, and assist youths aging out of foster care with independent living skills and support. The amount of money that states receive from this funding stream, especially funds for foster care, has steadily decreased over time because the income criteria that determines whether children's expenses are reimbursable by the federal government has remained unchanged in almost two decades. Thus, as the cost of living and the federal poverty line have increased, the funds available to states from the federal government have decreased (DeVooght et al., 2012). This is critical, as these foster care funds are used not only to cover living expenses for children in foster care but also to fund child welfare caseworker training and positions. With steadily decreasing federal funds, states rely on state and local government funds and other related programs such as Medicaid and Temporary Assistance to Needy Families to fund child welfare services. Thus, when examining potential gubernatorial and mayoral candidates, it is vital to make sure that whoever is elected is committed to funding these programs, as this will provide agencies with more funds for child welfare services.

In addition, the federal government is giving states the opportunity to receive certain funds with the flexibility to allocate them for different services, allowing states to pay for evidence-supported interventions that may have previously been underfunded. One such example is Pennsylvania and its participation in the Title IV-E Waiver Demonstration Project. This project provided the opportunity for county child welfare agencies in the state to use Title IV-E funds at their discretion. Counties in Pennsylvania were then able to adopt three evidence-based treatments for children and families in the child welfare system that they were previously unable to implement due to lack of funding. The waiver funds have allowed the state to train child welfare caseworkers, develop databases to track outcomes of children and families, and train staff to use local data to inform practice. The Title IV-E Waiver Demonstration Project was a provision in the Child and Family Services Improvement and Innovation Act, which was reauthorized for five years in 2011 (DeVooght et al., 2012). This act will be eligible for reauthorization

in 2016, which means that Congress will have the ability to implement changes in the way child welfare federal funds are allocated.
This is an opportunity for you, as a voter, to contact your congressional representative and senator to advocate for states to continue having the ability to redistribute federal funds and expand this program
so that more states will have the opportunity to reallocate funds and
promote child safety.

Sources

Aarons, G.A., Hurlburt, M., & Horwitz, S. (2011). "Advancing a conceptual
   model of evidence-based practice implementation in public service sectors." *Administration and Policy in Mental Health and Mental Health Services Research*, 38, 4–23.
Bowen, S., Erickson, T., Martens, P. J., & Crockett, S. (2009). More than "using
   research": The real challenges in promoting evidence-informed decision-
   making. *Healthcare Policy*, 4(3), 87–102.
Buckley, H., Tonmyr, L., Lewig, K., & Jack, S. (2014). Factors influencing the
   uptake of research evidence in child welfare: A synthesis of findings from
   Australia, Canada and Ireland. *Child Abuse Review*, 23(1), 5–16.
Child Welfare League of America. (2001). *Caseload and Workload Management*. Available from https://www.childwelfare.gov/pubPDFs/case_work
   _management.pdf
Collins-Camargo, C., McBeath, B., & Ensign, K. (2011). Privatization and
   performance-based contracting in child welfare: Recent trends and implications for social service administrators. *Administration in Social Work*,
   35(5), 494–516.
Day, P., & Peterson, C. (2008). Caseload reduction efforts in selected states.
   Unpublished manuscript, Casey Family Programs and ICF International.
DeVooght, K., Fletcher, M., Vaughn, B., & Cooper, H. (2012). Federal, state,
   and local spending to address child abuse and neglect in SFYs 2008 and
   2010. Washington, DC: Child Trends. Retrieved March, 18, 2013.
Fang, X., Brown, D. S., Florence, C. S., & Mercy, J. A. (2012). The economic
   burden of child maltreatment in the United States and implications for
   prevention. *Child Abuse & Neglect*, 36(2), 156–65.
Fedoravicius, N., McMillen, J. C., Rowe, J. E., Kagotho, N., & Ware, N. C.
   (2008). Funneling child welfare consumers into and through the mental

health system: Assessment, referral, and quality issues. *Social Service Review, 82*(2), 273–90.

Garcia, A. R., Circo, E., DeNard, C., & Hernandez, N. (2015). Barriers and facilitators to delivering mental health practice strategies for youth and families served by the child welfare system. *Children and Youth Services Review, 52,* 110–22.

Garcia, A. R., Palinkas, L. A., Snowden, L., & Landsverk, J. (2013). Looking beneath and in-between the hidden surfaces: A critical review of defining, measuring and contextualizing mental health service disparities in the child welfare system. *Children and Youth Services Review, 35* (10), 1727–33.

Palinkas, L.A., Fuentes, D., Finno, M., Garcia, A.R., Holloway, I.W., & Chamberlain, P. (2014). Inter-organizational collaboration in the implementation of evidence-based practices among public agencies serving abused and neglected youth. *Administration and Policy in Mental Health and Mental Health Services Research, 41*(1), 74-85.

Self, J. (2014). 40% of SC child-welfare workers bear heavy caseloads. *The Buzz.* Accessed at http://www.thestate.com/news/politics-government/politics-columns-blogs/the-buzz/article13864100.html.

Stiffman, A. R., Pescosolido, B., & Cabassa, L. J. (2004). Building a model to understand youth service access: The gateway provider model. *Mental Health Services Research, 6*(4), 189–98.

U.S. Department of Health and Human Services, Administration for Children and Families, Administration on Children, Youth and Families, Children's Bureau. (2011). *Child Maltreatment 2010.*

———. (2014). *Preliminary Estimates for FY 2013.*

CHAPTER 4

Substance Use, Incarceration,
and Homelessness

Mapping and Navigating Intersecting Risk Environments

Toorjo Ghose

Frequent episodes of incarceration, substance use, and homelessness are intersecting factors that contribute to the risk environment
for poor people of color residing in urban settings in the United
States. The war on drugs has resulted in the United States holding
the dubious record for the largest incarcerated population in the
world and indeed the largest at any point of time in history. While
substance use is the most significant risk factor for incarceration,
episodic periods of imprisonment result in unstable housing and
homelessness over the long-term, which in turn are closely correlated with substance use and recidivism. These overlapping cycles
of risk create multiple barriers for poor people of color residing in
inner-city settings. Policies and interventions addressing these risks
seldom account for the multidimensional nature of the problem,
and indeed, piecemeal strategies often result in exacerbating one
risk while addressing another. Moreover, existing governmental
bureaucracies discourage the forging of a comprehensive solution
by maintaining organizational silos whereby resources invested by

one section (housing, for instance) reap benefits only for others (mental health and primary care). Harsher critics have highlighted the neoliberal impulse driving what they refer to as the prison-industrial complex, whereby policies maintain the cycle in order to fuel the market spawned by people (and capital) passing through the revolving door of prisons. Finally, service provision at the individual level often ignores structural factors and the multithreaded fabric of the risk environment swaddling communities. I seek to map the manner in which substance use, homelessness, and incarceration interact with each other as well as the manner in which service provision and policies are falling short in their attempt to address these issues. I also draw on my current research and policy work with governments in the United States and other countries to identify a multilevel approach to this issue—one that collaboratively engages the community at the street level to provide group and collective-based services as well as advocacy while simultaneously engaging the policy processes at the governmental level to establish comprehensive policy solutions.

Incarceration, Homelessness, and Risk Behaviors: The Research Evidence

Incarceration and homelessness. Homelessness and incarceration appear to have a bidirectional relationship: a history of incarceration raises the risk of homelessness and vice versa (Kushel et al., 2005). A study on patients released from a midwestern state hospital found that involvement with the law was associated with later homelessness (Belcher et al., 1988). Elevated rates of substance abuse among those incarcerated increase the risk of homelessness and the need for services postrelease. In a sample of 165 jailed women in Ohio, Alemagno (2001) found that 81% of women who reported needing substance abuse services also reported needing housing services after release, compared to 45% of women who did not need substance abuse treatment. Similarly, substance-using women were more likely to report needing medical and mental health services at significantly higher rates than women who did not need substance abuse treatment services.

Homelessness and the behavioral risk environments: Substance use, homelessness, and HIV risk. Aidala and colleagues (2005) found that in a sample of HIV-positive subjects, the risk of hard drug use, needle sharing, engaging in unprotected sex, and exchanging sex for money were three to six times higher among the homeless than among the stably housed. Change in housing status was also significantly correlated with HIV risk factors. Improved housing stability significantly reduced the risk of hard drug use, needle sharing, engaging in sex for money, and unprotected sex. Similarly, in a sample of African American male intravenous drug users, homeless subjects were more than twice as likely to share needles, have multiple sex partners, and engage in unprotected sex (Salazar et al., 2005). In a national study of syringe exchange programs in the United States, Des Jarlais, Braine, and Friedmann (2007) found that on average, unstably housed exchange participants were more than twice as likely as stably housed participants to report continued high-risk syringe sharing. Examining HIV risk practices in a sample of injection drug users, Sethi and colleagues (2004) found that unstable housing significantly increased the risk of sharing dirty needles and engaging in sex work.

Violence, homelessness and risky behaviors. Scholars have documented high levels of physical and sexual violence among homeless women (Burt, Aron, & Lee, 2001; Henry et al., 2007), especially those with a history of incarceration (Hudson et al., 2010). Living on the streets and in shelters exposes women to such levels of violence that sexual assault is almost normative for homeless women (Goodman, Dutton, & Harris, 1995). Studies have also found that sexual trauma and post-traumatic stress disorder among homeless women result in high levels of impulsivity, risky substance use, and risky sexual practices (Burt, Aron, & Lee, 2011; Henry et al., 2007; Aidala, Abramson, & Lee, 2001). The studies indicate that homelessness creates an unsafe context that results in substance use, use of needles, involuntary and violent sexual encounters, and engagement in unsafe sexual practices.

Housing and utilization of health care services. Scholars have found that the homeless and the unstably housed are less likely to receive medical care (Aidala et al., 2001a; Aidala et al., 2007; Aidala et al., 2001b). In a national study on health care service utilization, homelessness significantly reduced the likelihood of entering into medical care as well as receiving appropriate HIV care (Aidala et al., 2007). In a review of scholarship on the link between housing and health services utilization, Leaver et al. (2007) found that the homeless were less likely to use primary care and ambulatory services. On the other hand, scholars have found that homeless subjects were more likely to use more expensive services such as emergency care (Arno et al., 1996) and hospitalization (Smith et al., 2000). In the Housing and Health Study, Kidder and colleagues (2007) found that homelessness almost doubled the risk of subjects using emergency room services to meet basic health needs. Examining a housing program run by New York City, Culhane, Metraux, and Hadley (2002) found that compared to the homeless, housed subjects on average reduced their stays in shelters and state hospitals by 153 and 75 days, respectively.

Despite the considerable evidence demonstrating the overlap of homelessness, incarceration, and risk behaviors, the service delivery system seldom addresses these challenges simultaneously. Barriers to a comprehensive conceptualization of the problem and its solutions are embedded in both the policy realm and the service delivery landscape.

Barriers to an Effective Solution

The challenge of the new policy environment. The Affordable Care Act (ACA) has reshaped how agencies will be operating in the future. In particular, private insurance has become more central to the reimbursement process, and agencies are now discouraged from catering to particular or specialized populations unless they are part of a network that provides care to the general population. While the ACA constitutes a giant step forward in trying to establish universal health care in the United States, these two aspects of the law may have detrimental and unwanted side effects for the vulnerable populations we are concerned with. First, in the new era of muscular private insurance driven by the dictates of cost-effectiveness, agencies will be tempted to explore cost-cutting measures such as eliminating their costliest clients, or those who require the highest level of care. This process, known as "creaming," threatens to disproportionately target clients with a history of homelessness, substance use, and incarceration, since they constitute the section of frequent service users who drive up costs for providers.

Second, in the new era of generalized and universal care, the specialized care that this population may require might also be put on the chopping block. Historically, care for marginalized populations has had to be carved out of protocols of services provided to the general population. Treatment as usual provided by clinicians who were often insensitive to the needs of this community seldom addressed the complex psychosocial matrix of challenges confronting clients. In fact, it has often taken a social movement to establish effective health care for communities such as the homeless, injection drug users, people living with HIV, and gay, lesbian, bisexual, and transgender clients. The ACA, with its stipulations to service providers to move away from serving the needs of particular communities, assumes that stigmatized, discriminated against, and vulnerable groups such as those with a history of incarceration, substance use, and homelessness will receive adequate care in the general service system. However, there is no evidence to show that the system, which proved to be inadequate in meeting the needs of these communities in the past, has gained the capability to do so now.

The conundrum of silos. At the federal, state, and city levels, governmental departments oversee the various areas of health services that are pertinent to our population in question. Thus, housing, mental and physical health, criminal justice, employment, and welfare are housed in separate departments, all of which coordinate services for clients with a history of homelessness, substance use, and incarceration. In theory, these departments are in conversation with each other. However, without an explicit and comprehensive strategy to integrate initiatives among them, the collaboration needed for effective services is often absent. Budgets too are seldom coordinated, with no incentives for one department to invest resources when another will benefit from the costs saved down the line. Effective mental health or housing services for instance, might result in reduced incarceration episodes and hospital emergency room visits, ensuring that the greatest savings in costs will be enjoyed by the criminal justice and health departments rather than the departments of housing and mental health. The challenges confronted by this population are seldom restricted to specialty areas and require a governmental structure that is able to mount a coordinated response to them.

Challenges at the service provider level. Governmental silos often reproduce themselves on the ground, with service providers addressing issues separately. While substance use treatment providers have made efforts in recent years to integrate mental health treatment into their menu of services, housing, employment, legal services, and support for reintegration into the community are usually not part of the treatment protocol. Moreover, while the ACA encourages the establishment of provider networks, currently most agencies on the ground have limited relationships with each other.

One of the biggest barriers to service provision in this population is the difficulty in ensuring access to treatment and retaining clients over the long term. While clients with a history of homelessness, incarceration, and substance use constitute the section of clientele that requires the highest level of care, treatment coverage is extremely poor in this population. Without a strategy to circumvent these challenges of access and retention, all interventions with this group of clients will ultimately fail.

The challenges described above present themselves at multiple levels in the treatment landscape and require a multilevel, multisystemic response.

Enunciating a Multilevel Solution

A comprehensive response to the intersecting environments of risk and need for this population necessitates addressing both the policy and the service-provision dimensions of the problems described above.

Policy initiatives. At a meeting convened by the White House's Office of National AIDS Policy in 2011, a committee formulating the national AIDS strategy recognized that there was considerable overlap among the formerly incarcerated, homeless, and substance using communities and that those at the intersection of these multiple risk environments constituted the most vulnerable population in the epidemic. As a participant of the committee, I draw on some of the recommendations that emerged from these discussions to formulate policy-level interventions to address the needs of this group. Specifically, I argue for the need to (1) foreground this population and its unique needs in the policy formulation process, (2) realign the way governmental departments work with each other to address these needs, and (3) implement shifts in legal policies regarding drugs and housing.

Keeping the focus on the most vulnerable. Policy needs to immediately address the dual threat of creaming and the elimination of specialized care that has been described above. While these challenges have always been part of the service provision landscape, the ACA incentivizes agencies to engage in these practices. Health policy makers will have to explicitly underline the need for services to populations with a history of homelessness, substance use, and incarceration. Funding and reimbursement guidelines need to ask for an evaluation of how this population has been retained and how their needs are addressed by agencies. Finally, the new forms of organizational structures described in the ACA (such as the creation of a network of service providers) need to include specialized providers who serve this population. Without these explicit stipulations, treatment as usual will eventually eliminate services for this community, and these vulnerable clients will continue to be stuck in the community-to-prison pipeline.

Busting departmental silos. An effective response to the intersecting matrix of risk described above entails the realignment of governmental departments and the redefinition of their relationship with each other. As part of the process of developing a national AIDS strategy, the White House Office of National AIDS Policy met in 2012 and emphasized the need for collaboration across governmental departments in order to address the needs of those most at risk. As part of those discussions, the author helped to craft a plan recommending the establishment of a cross-departmental committee charged with fostering collaborations across departments responsible for the welfare of vulnerable communities. Specifically, the committee would help to map out a comprehensive strategy to engage homeless substance users involved with the carceral system that would include departments such as housing, substance use, health and human services, and justice. A crucial element of this strategy would involve incentivizing the participation of departments by determining their share of the costs saved in successfully intervening with the community. For instance, the incentives associated with costs saved in reduced emergency room visits due to the provision of housing to homeless people released from prison would be shared with the departments of housing and criminal justice, offsetting the resources they would have invested in linking people with housing.

Implementing reform around drug laws and housing. Incarceration for marijuana-related charges accounts for a significant proportion of the prison and jail population in the United States. Recent city and statewide initiatives have succeeded in decriminalizing marijuana use in many areas of the country. However, the poorest sections of the population in cities such as Philadelphia continue to be subjected to arrests for marijuana use, despite the reform in laws. A significant step forward in reducing the risk environment confronting our population in question would be to enforce the new laws by ensuring that the police and local municipal court judges are acting within the bounds of the new legislation.

Housing interventions for the homeless constitute another area that has witnessed a shift in policy in recent years. Most housing interventions for substance users and the mentally ill make housing contingent on attending treatment and staying abstinent. Guided by recent research evidence, however, Housing First policies have come to the fore, whereby vulnerable clients retain their housing even if they do not remain abstinent or attend treatment. The Veterans

Affairs housing program, for instance, has started to implement a Housing First policy. As with marijuana use, however, the principles of Housing First can be easily subverted by program directors who disagree with the policy. Housing First, as a policy initiative, is a powerful means to sever the community-to-prison pipeline. Proper implementation will ensure the viability of this policy tool.

Service-related initiatives. In early 2015 in response to the service provision-related challenges described above, a group at the University of Pennsylvania's School of Social Policy & Practice (SP2) headed by the author established an agency called the Center for Carceral Communities to engage clients with a history of substance use, incarceration, and homelessness. I draw on the center's structures and processes to enunciate an initiative that responds to the barriers described above.

Most clients at the Center for Carceral Communities are unemployed and homeless when they come in. The center seeks to establish a one-stop wraparound triage and service facility that (1) engages clients in evidence-based interventions (EBIs) that address intersecting vectors of risk, (2) involves them in the decision-making processes of the agency so they become owners of the intervention process, and (3) advocates for structural changes in the carceral and service delivery systems by developing models of effective organizational processes and protocols.

Engaging in EBIs that address the risk environment. While EBI has become a fashionable term in the intervention and service-delivery community, implementing EBIs in the real world has proven to be a challenge for most agencies. Barriers to implementation include a dearth of trained clinical staff, the diversity of contexts that characterize the service-delivery environment, challenges associated with ensuring adherence to protocols, and the inability of most EBIs to comprehensively address the complicated risk factors confronting clients. The Center for Carceral Communities addresses these challenges by implementing an evidence-based protocol of group therapy called the CHATS intervention (for Challenges, Alternatives, Triumphs and Solutions) married to intensive case management for its clients. The CHATS model combines the common elements of various therapeutic modalities that have been shown to be effective in behavioral change in this population. Specifically, it draws group process as well as cognitive behavioral, motivational interviewing, and solution-focused therapeutic techniques to engage clients in behavior change. CHATS is flexible in its goals and simultaneously addresses issues such as mental health, substance use, employment, legal challenges, and engagement in health behaviors. As will be described later, CHATS is a structured, concrete protocol that allows clients to quickly become proficient in it in order to implement it in their own lives as well as help their peers to engage in it. Finally, in addition to CHATS, the Center for Carceral Communities engages clients in intensive case management that links them to housing, employment, legal support, and childcare. Training and evaluations are conducted by scholars at SP2 at Penn, allowing providers to have continuous access to clinical support, research, and outcomes.

Investing clients with ownership of the treatment process. One of the goals of CHATS intervention is to certify clients as cofacilitators of the protocol so that they enhance their employability as peer counselors. The goal of getting certified and eventually transitioning to cofacilitator status allows clients to own the treatment rather than always remaining the object of care. Moreover, cofacilitation serves as a powerful incentive to remain engaged in treatment. The ownership of treatment is enhanced by the fact that clients are included in management meetings and decisions. Finally, clients volunteer to become ambassadors of the Center for Carceral Communities, making presentations to various audiences such as judges, agency heads, and community college students on issues pertinent to them.

Advocating for systemic change. One of the goals of the Center for Carceral Communities is to establish a network of providers who are engaged in similar practices for this population of clients. The center works closely with several agencies with a similar mission and is also currently training personnel from other agencies in the CHATS model as well as in its organizational practices. A version of the multitiered intervention model is being pilot-tested by New York City's Department of Health and Mental Health in agencies across the city as part of its initiative to end AIDS by 2020. The longer-term goal of the initiative is to advocate for evidence-based change in the treatment system by modeling innovative processes that address the challenges described above and examining their effectiveness.

Conclusion

People with a history of incarceration, homelessness, and substance use constitute the most vulnerable section of clients in any treatment system. Their needs are multifaceted, warranting a comprehensive, multilevel, and multisystemic approach to meeting them. This chapter describes these challenges as well as a possible approach to solving them (Figure 1). Effective interventions

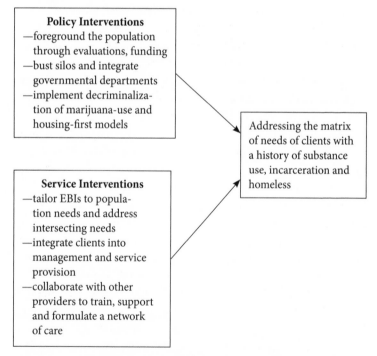

Figure 1. A multilevel intervention plan for people with a history of substance use, incarceration, and homelessness.

with this community will have a significant impact on health disparities, reincarceration rates, homelessness, physical as well as mental health, and health care costs. It is well worth the effort to forge an effective response to the challenges that this community faces, one that is predicated on a close collaboration among partners in the academy, in the policy sphere, and in service-providing agencies.

Sources

Aidala, A., Cross, J. E., Stall, R., Harre, D., & Sumartojo, E. (2005). Housing status and HIV risk behaviors: Implications for prevention and policy. *AIDS and Behavior, 34,* 251–65.

Aidala, A. A., Davis, N., Abramson, D., & Lee, G. (2001). *Housing status and health outcomes among persons living with HIV/AIDS.* New York: Columbia University Press.

Aidala, A. A., Gunjeong, L., Abramson, D., Messeri, P., & Siegler, A. (2007). Housing need, housing assistance and connection to HIV medical care. *AIDS and Behavior, 11,* Supplement 2, S101–S115.

Aidala, A. A., Messeri, P., Abramson, D., & Lee, G. (2001). *Housing and health care among persons living with HIV/AIDS.* New York: Columbia University Press.

Alemagno, S. A. (2001). Women in jail: Is substance abuse treatment enough? *American Journal of Public Health, 91,* 798–800.

Arno, P. S., Bonuck, K. A., Green, J., Fleishman, J., Bennett, C. L., Fahs, M. C., Maffeo, C., & Drucker, E. (1996). The impact of housing status on health care utilization among persons with HIV disease. *Journal of Health Care Poor Underserved, 7*(1), 36–49.

Belcher, J. R. (1988). Are jails replacing the mental health system for the homeless mentally ill? *Community Mental Health Journal, 24,* 185–95.

Burt, M., Aron, L., & Lee, E. (2001). *Helping America's homeless: Emergency shelter or affordable housing?* Washington, DC: Urban Institute Press.

Culhane, D. P., Metraux, S., & Hadley, T. R. (2002). Public service reductions associated with the placement of homeless people with severe mental illness in supportive housing. *Housing Policy Debate, 13,* 107–63.

Des Jarlais, D. C., Braine, N., & Friedmann, P. (2007). Unstable housing as a factor for increased injection risk behavior at US syringe exchange programs. *AIDS & Behavior, 11,* Supplement 2, S78–S84.

Goodman, L. A., Dutton, M. A., & Harris, M. (1995). Episodically homeless women with serious mental illness: Prevalence of physical and sexual assault. *American Journal of Orthopsychiatry, 65*(4), 468–78.

Henny, K. D., Kidder, D. P., Stall, R., & Wolitsky, R. J. (2007). Physical and sexual abuse among homeless and unstably housed adults living with HIV: Prevalence and associated risks. *AIDS & Behavior, 11*, 842–53.

Hudson, A. L., Wright, K., Bhattacharya, D., Sinha, K., Nyamathi, A., et al. (2010). Correlates of adult assault among homeless women. *Journal of Health Care for the Poor and Underserved, 21*(4), 1250–62.

Kidder, D. P., Wolitski, R. J., Campsmith, M. L., & Nakamura, G. V. (2007). Health status, health care use, medication use, and medication adherence among homeless and housed people living with HIV/AIDS. *American Journal of Public Health, 97*, 2238–45.

Kushel, M. B., Hahn, J. A., Evans, J. L., Bangsberg, D. R., & Moss, A. R. (2005). Revolving doors: Imprisonment among the homeless and marginally housed population. *American Journal of Public Health, 95*(10), 1747–52.

Leaver, C., Bargh, G., Dung, J., & Hwang, S. (2007). The effects of housing status on health-related outcomes in people living with HIV: A systematic review of the literature. *AIDS & Behavior, 11*, Supplement 2, 85–100.

Salazar, L. F., Cosby, R. A., Holtgrave, D. R., Head, S., Hadsock, B., Todd, J., et al. (2005). Homelessness and HIV-associated risk behavior among African American men who inject drugs and reside in the urban south of the United States. *AIDS and Behavior, 9*, 266–74.

Sethi, A. K., Celentano, D. D., Gange, S. J., Gallant, J. E., Vlahov, D., & Farzadegan, H. (2004). High-risk behavior and potential transmission of drug-resistant HIV among injection drug users. *Journal of Acquired Immune Deficiency Syndromes, 35*(5), 503–10.

Smith, M. Y., Rapkin, B. D., Winkel, G., Springer, C., Chhabra, R., & Feldman, I. S. (2000). Housing status and health care service utilization among low-income persons with HIV/AIDS. *Journal of General Internal Medicine, 15*(10), 731–38.

CHAPTER 5

Foster Care, Then Where?

Why Independent Living Is Getting It All Wrong

Johanna Greeson and Allison Thompson

Comparing Experiences

Imagine that you are an average young person in your mid-20s living in the 1960s. Chances are, you and the majority of your peers are financially self-sufficient and living outside of your parents' home, either independently with a partner or married. Many of you will also have children by now. Most likely, you didn't go to college but are still able to make a livable wage of approximately $31,000 per year. You've probably decided your career path and will likely stick with it for some time. Out of 10 of your friends, only 1 has a college degree. This friend probably only makes about $7,000 more than you each year. It is relatively common for you and your same-aged friends to be homeowners and quite unusual for any of your peers to still live with parents.

Now fast-forward 50 years to the 2010s and place yourself in the shoes of an average young person in his or her mid-20s. You likely still live with your parents and report your financial situation as less than good. You've felt pressure to attend college because you know that the chances of living in poverty if you don't are one in four. In fact, 40% of your same-aged peers also enroll in college, because with a degree they earn roughly 60% more than your friends without one. Among those of you who live with your parents, almost half are unemployed, and 82% of Americans believe that it is harder for your generation to find jobs than it was for your parents. Though most of your young friends are not the heads of their households, those who are likely possess assets that total no more than $33,000 compared to other heads of households over 35 years of age, whose average assets total over $230,000.

Finally, imagine that you're a young person in your 20s who exited foster care in the 2010s. It is likely you are living alone, though between you and your 2 friends at least 1 of you has experienced homelessness since you left foster care. You probably have a high school diploma but not a college degree. In fact, of the 20 people who exited foster care with you, only 1 has completed a two- or four-year college program. Though it is likely that you are working or have worked, it is also likely that you are living in poverty, as your average earnings per year are only $8,000. Your friends who have never lived in foster care make $4 per hour more than you. You have experienced material hardship, such as a utility shut-off or eviction, and 1 in 3 of your friends has inconsistent access to enough food. It is likely that you rely on needs-based government help, such as food stamps and cash assistance, to survive.

As a young person who exited foster care without a legally binding, permanent connection to a family, you have aged out of care. You recall the path that you took over the past 10 years leading to your current situation. You first entered foster care when you were 12 years old, and after a couple of years it became clear that you were unable to return home to your parents. Your county caseworker tried to reassure you, saying that it was her job to find you a "forever family." Four foster homes, three group homes, six schools, and eight caseworkers later, you are told that it would be better for you to work toward "independent living." You have been failed by the system. When you are 17 years old none of your former foster parents want you to live with them, and your group home says that you can't stay past your 18th birthday. You are told that you will live by yourself in an apartment. Your caseworker suggests that you start taking classes to acquire the daily living skills necessary for success. It all feels strange to you, as life in the group home provided anything but a normative experience. You were told when to wake up, when and what to eat, and when to go to bed. You have never spent the night at a friend's house and grabbed an after-school snack, nor do you have a driver's license. While in the group home you never went grocery shopping, let alone budgeted for meals or even cooked a dinner. The classes you took only gave you a vague understanding of what it meant to make it alone.

Almost overnight you are placed in an apartment in yet another new neighborhood, separated again from the few adults who have become important to you. You are told that you have to maintain a job or enroll in school, and you take three buses one way to complete the hour-and-a-half commute to work a minimum wage job. You take night classes part-time at the local community college.

Three years fly by, and now you are 21. You are on your own, the family court judge tells you. You have aged out of care. The state will no longer provide an apartment for you or support your education, although you haven't completed your degree. The state, which has legally been your parent for the past decade, abruptly ends all support when you turn 21. The state failed at finding a "forever family" for you as it promised years ago.

You feel angry when you think about the financial support and privilege many young people in their 20s receive from their parents compared to what has been expected of you. Instead of rushing from classes to a job, you would like to be able to live in a college dorm, have the opportunity to engage in fun conversations, and build relationships with your peers. These peers, who are living out the "ideal" college experience, are undergoing an exciting time of exploration, one in which most are afforded the full benefits of parental provision and support without the restrictions of parental supervision and control. They are encouraged to delay the adoption of adult roles and to gradually enter adulthood at a pace that best supports their exploration of work, love, and meaning. For them, it is a time that has been referred to as independent exploration. But as an independent youth formerly in foster care, your reality is different. For you it is more appropriate to refer to this period of time as one of independent survival.

Why Independent Living Does Not Work

As a society, we need to reconsider why each year 1 in 10 youths is encouraged to exit foster care to live independently. Times have changed since the 1960s. Even among the most motivated and hardworking, our current economy doesn't permit the majority of young people to obtain livable wages, purchase affordable housing, and support a family at the age of 21. Financial, residential, and familial independence are associated with one's passage into adulthood, and young people today continue to delay this passage well into their 20s and even 30s. They increasingly rely on their families for support, and nearly half of all young people who leave home will end up returning at some point.

If we do not expect young people with supportive families and plentiful opportunities to function independently in their 20s, why do we assume that young people who have experienced trauma, maltreatment, disrupted relationships, instability, and social isolation should be independent? What happens to young people who have exited foster care when they do not have a family to return to? What happens when they are forced to take on adult roles but are unready to live independently? In the absence of the support that most emerging adults in the general population experience, young people formerly in foster care become dependent on the only systems of "support" available: criminal justice, welfare, low-income housing, and mental and behavioral health. In fact, it is estimated that on average for every young person who ages out of foster care, taxpayers and communities pay $300,000 in social costs over that person's lifetime. With approximately 26,000 young people aging out each year, this amounts to nearly $8 billion in total costs. We must reconceptualize independent living for young people aging out of foster care. Independent living does not work.

A Reconceptualization

We are calling for a reconceptualization of *independent* living to *interdependent* living. The term "independent living" usually refers to an individual's ability to be self-sufficient and self-reliant. In contrast, we use the term "interdependent living" to describe an individual's need to live in close relationship with others and depend on others to provide support while also contributing to others' overall well-being. Such support can take many different forms and usually includes emotional support and guidance, informational support, and tangible support, such as financial help, housing assistance, and material goods. Similar to young people in the general population who rely on their families for support late into their 20s, young people formerly in foster care may experience improved lives with the help of strong social support networks, including the presence of at least one caring, committed adult who is not their parent. Such nonparental supportive adults are sometimes referred to as natural mentors because these adults naturally serve as mentors, often without being formally labeled as such. Natural mentors may include teachers, religious leaders, neighbors, aunts and uncles, and even professional caseworkers and therapists who continue to maintain a relationship after a young person leaves their formal service.

A growing body of research and testimonials from young people formerly in foster care support a reconceptualization of independent to interdependent living. This makes sense intuitively. Think back over your life. Can you identify natural mentors who believed in you? How did they support you and contribute to your achievements and successes? These relationships often span over time and help us weather the storms of life. In this way they can be *permanent* relationships, even if a court has not legally declared it so. Natural mentoring may also help youths who have experienced instability, as natural mentors may serve as a rare constant in the lives of youths experiencing foster care drift, or movement from home to home. Relationships with natural mentors can have a lasting impact in the lives of young people who have exited foster care. Such is the case with writer Antwone Fisher, whose story about aging out of foster care as a young person was made into a Hollywood film starring Denzel Washington. In his book *Finding Fish: A Memoir*, Fisher describes his transition to a new school, where he met a wonderful teacher, a woman he considers to be a key mentor in his life:

> With a new name and enrollment in a different school, I was given a chance to start over—to reinvent myself. And a big part of the new me was a woman by the name of Mrs. Profit, a teacher in the truest and best sense of the word. If there is such a thing as human beings who act as angels in our lives, Brenda Profit was that for me. . . . Brenda Profit became more than a teacher to me; in fact, she was the woman closest to a mother that I would ever know. . . . As if in answer to prayers I hadn't even prayed, Mrs. Profit started addressing many of my concerns in school. She devoted a portion of health class not only to those more specific explanations of where babies came from, but also to general things like how to take a bath and groom oneself. The fact that she talked about things that related directly to me made me pay more attention to the other subjects that were still very foreign. . . . By day, my life with Mrs. Profit and the rest of my family at school gave me breathing room. (Fisher, 2001, pp. 123–33)

Looking Forward: A Promising Practice

Though natural mentoring relationships exist organically within young people's social networks, these relationships may still benefit from programmatic support. Such programs may be useful in several ways. For example, some youths may need help recognizing potential natural mentors within their social networks. Youths sometimes say that they don't have supportive adults in their lives, but they may just require assistance identifying and approaching potentially supportive adults. Other youths may readily identify natural mentors but still benefit from relationship support. Such support could help the youth/mentor pairs clarify expectations for the relationship after foster care or deal with brewing conflict before it explodes. In fact, the latest *Handbook on Youth Mentoring* recognizes the potential support that natural mentors provide for youths exiting care and recommends that child welfare agencies systematically rally and include natural mentors in the transition planning process for older youths at risk of aging out of foster care. Consistent with this recommendation, Caring Adults 'R' Everywhere (C.A.R.E.) is a novel natural mentoring child welfare-based intervention intended to support interdependence among older youths at risk of aging out of care.

C.A.R.E. is a 12-week manualized intervention developed by Dr. Johanna Greeson of the University of Pennsylvania. Designed to promote lasting relationships between older youths in foster care and their natural mentors, C.A.R.E. is theory driven and research supported. Prior to the start of the intervention, a master's-level trained interventionist assists youths to self-select and identify potential adults who may serve as natural mentors. Once the adults are identified, screened, and approved, they receive trauma-informed natural mentor training. The training includes information about adolescent human development, the impact of trauma on development, effective strategies for mentoring, and mentor self-care. During the heart of the intervention, the interventionist meets with the youth/natural mentor pairs each week to support the development of their relationships. The pairs also spend intentional weekly time in the community to work on life skills development in a more natural context. For example, rather than learning about meal preparation in a classroom setting, the youth and the natural mentor develop a grocery list and budget, shop, prepare the meal, and enjoy food and conversation together. There are also large group activities designed to provide a community of support among the youths and the natural mentors. Throughout the intervention, the pairs video-record their experiences to memorialize the development of their relationships; the videos are then showcased and celebrated during a formal gathering at the end of the intervention. Booster sessions, or aftercare, are available as needed after the completion of the 12-week intervention. C.A.R.E. is currently being piloted in partnership with the Philadelphia's Department of Human Services.

Programs such as C.A.R.E. that support interdependent living among older youths exiting foster care are quite rare. Sadly, independent living programs dominate practice for aging out youths even as research shows that these services are ineffective in preparing youths for life after foster care. Recent research also suggests that independent living programs do not increase or strengthen social supports for youths exiting the system. Yet for the past three decades, federal dollars have financed independent living programs. Since 2002, unsuccessful attempts have been made by every session of Congress to pass a Foster Care Mentoring Act, which would direct federal dollars toward mentoring programs for youths in foster care. New federal legislation is needed to mandate that independent living services be replaced with interdependent living services in the form of natural mentoring interventions, such as C.A.R.E., for this high-risk population of young people. Rather than funneling money toward services that do not work, we need to rethink how we can better serve young people aging out of foster care by supporting the interdependence between them and caring, supportive adults.

Such interdependent policy and practice represents a shift away from the traditional model, which focuses on targeting individual-level skill building to promote self-sufficiency rather than strengthening the social networks of youths. We urge you to join us in reconceptualizing independent living to interdependent living for older youths aging out of the foster care system. Let's stop expecting youths to *independently* survive and start helping them *interdependently* thrive.

Sources

Arnett, J. J. (2014). *Emerging adulthood: The winding road from the late teens through the twenties.* New York: Oxford University Press.

Britner, P. A., Randall, K. G., & Ahrens, K. R. (2013). Youth in foster care. In D. L. DuBois & M. J. Karcher (Eds.), *The handbook of youth mentoring,* pp. 341–54. Thousand Oaks, CA: Sage.

Courtney, M. E., Zinn, A., Johnson, H., & Malm, K. E. (2011). *Evaluation of the Massachusetts adolescent outreach program for youths in intensive foster care: Final report (Vol. 14); OPRE Report 2011-14.*

Courtney, M. E., Zinn, A., Koralek, R. & Bess, R. J. (2011). *Evaluation of the independent living—Employment services program, Kern County, California: Final report; OPRE report, 2011-13.*

Foster Care Independent Act of 1999, Pub. L. No. 106-169, § 101, 113 Stat. 1824.

Greeson, J. K. P. (2013). Foster youth and the transition to adulthood: The theoretical and conceptual basis for natural mentoring. *Emerging Adulthood, 1*(1), 40–51.

Greeson, J. K. P., Garcia, A. R., Kim, M., & Courtney, M. E. (2014). Foster youth and social support: The first RCT of independent living services. *Research on Social Work Practice.*

Jim Casey Youth Opportunities Initiative (2012). *Cost avoidance: The business case for investing in youth aging out foster care.*

Propp, J., Ortega, D., & NewHeart, F. (2003). Independence or interdependence: Rethinking the transition from ward of the court to adulthood. *Families in Society, 84*(2), 259–66.

Data for vignettes taken from the following:

Pew Research Center, Social & Demographic Trends. (2013a). "A rising share of young adults live in their parents' home." Washington, DC: Pew Research Center.

———. (2013b). "Young adults after the recession: Fewer homes, fewer cars, less debt." Washington, DC: Pew Research Center.

———. (2014a). "Median annual earnings of 25–32 year olds, by educational attainment." Washington, DC: Pew Research Center.

———. (2014b). "The rising cost of not going to college." Washington, DC: Pew Research Center.

CHAPTER 6

The Reality of Urban Food Deserts and What Low-Income Food Shoppers Need

Amy Hillier and Benjamin Chrisinger

> You know, when I moved here, they told me that
> there was no supermarket in Chester. I was like,
> "You got to be kidding me. There's not a market
> here, in Chester?"
> —Chester, Pennsylvania, resident

Chester, Pennsylvania, is home to a relatively new casino and professional soccer stadium, both of which received public subsidies, but no supermarket. The high rate of food insecurity contributed to this city outside Philadelphia, Pennsylvania, earning the dubious distinction of being part of the nation's second-hungriest congressional district.

Many residents remember a thriving Chester with multiple supermarkets and neighborhood grocery stores stocked with fresh foods. Deindustrialization was as cruel to Chester as many other thriving cities. Between 1950 and 1990 Chester lost almost half its population, as nearly all its White residents left for the suburbs or other regions of the country. With the loss of industry, jobs, and people came the loss of supermarkets. By 2001 the last supermarket closed, leaving 38,000 residents to shop at corner stores and small grocers within the city or travel to the chain supermarkets in the suburbs.

Low-income residents in Chester describe the reality of shopping for fresh food in such an environment: "I am sad that we can't get any fresh produce in Chester, in the corner store, nothing fresh. Everything is in the can. I might just want to get some broccoli. I got to go to [a suburban supermarket] for some broccoli. It's crazy!" And "Only the corner store will have bananas; that's about it, and potatoes. But what you gonna do with bananas and potatoes all the time?"

Residents also express low expectations of the quality of food in local stores. A resident who shops for food at one of the several chain dollar stores in Chester describes purchasing a two-pound pack of cheese for a dollar: "Cheap and already expired. I tried to make a grilled cheese, and the cheese just spoiled." Others discuss the difficulty of getting to suburban supermarkets and depending on friends and relatives for rides or relying on the limited public transportation system. Depending on others means waiting, shopping where it is convenient for others, and lacking a sense of control over such a basic part of their lives. Those who rely on the bus mention spending 45 minutes to an hour just to get to a supermarket. "It is truly, truly a struggle," said one resident.

Traveling to find fresh food is only one nutrition-related challenge facing low-income households in Chester. Even with nutritional awareness, Chester residents face an uphill battle for their health. When residents travel to suburban supermarkets for healthful foods, the cost can be prohibitive. "I see it on TV all the time, Dr. Oz, all these people," comments one woman. "Well you just need to get one cup of avocado, blah, blah, blah, this, that. We can't afford it! How the hell . . . are we supposed to get healthy if we don't have healthy food available at a reduced price and/or available at food banks?"

The story of Philadelphia is better known but similar to Chester. These two cities, Chester and Philadelphia, are the sites of our research on food shopping and access to healthful food where we have worked closely with food retailers and food assistance program administrators. Most of what we have learned comes from listening to low-income food shoppers through surveys, focus groups, and in-depth interviews conducted in people's homes and at food stores where they shop. In this chapter, we reflect on the lessons learned from a series of separate research studies in the context of the larger policy and research discussions about what has come to be known as food deserts.

The Fascination with Food Deserts

Researchers and public officials in the United Kingdom started describing areas with limited supermarket access as food deserts in the 1990s, and a similar interest emerged in the United States a decade later. Early studies focused on the connection between being an underserved community with high rates of diet-related diseases, such as obesity, diabetes, and hypertension. One interpretation of this research was that if people lack access to healthy foods, they are more likely to have an unhealthy diet. Institutions from the *New York Times* to the National Institutes of Health to the White House all placed stock in this concept of food deserts and a national imperative to intervene.

Since the food desert concept entered public consciousness, an array of interdisciplinary research has complicated our assumptions about food access and health outcomes. Nevertheless, the term "food desert" accomplishes much. It draws attention to distinct and dramatic racial and economic inequalities in accessing healthy, affordable foods, especially produce. It resonates with a variety of stakeholder groups and engenders coalitions to bring new supermarkets into specific communities. Finally, it is instrumental in attracting hundreds of millions of development dollars to underserved areas—urban, suburban, and rural—around the nation.

Despite the usefulness of the food desert concept, it has notable shortcomings. First, as a spatial concept it does not address how people actually shop. In reality, the distance from a store to home is only one of many considerations when purchasing groceries. Second, the concept is deficit-oriented, meaning it focuses on what is absent from a community rather than what exists. Alternative food production and distribution channels, like community gardens, may exist in food deserts but are typically overlooked because of the term's focus on traditional retailers. Finally, the concept tends to imply a specific solution: develop a supermarket. Not only does this obscure the difficult issue of developing large retailers in lower-income communities, it also overlooks the more basic challenge of shopping while poor. Presumably, if communities had more money available for food shopping, retailers would willingly pursue nearby sites for development, eliminating food deserts on their own. Even still, supermarkets open and close based on local, regional, and international trends; thus, building a new store is far from a guaranteed long-term solution to a food desert.

Much of what we have learned in Chester and Philadelphia has defied common assumptions about food shopping embedded in the food desert concept as well as common stereotypes of low-income food deserts.

What We Know About Food Shopping and Food Environments in Low-Income Communities

1. *Most people, even low-income people, do most of their food shopping at supermarkets.* We found this to be true across race, income, and neighborhoods in Philadelphia. In North Philadelphia among African Americans and Puerto Ricans, 90% of women receiving benefits from the Special Supplemental Nutrition Program for Women, Infants, and Children (WIC) primarily shop at supermarkets. In West Philadelphia, 95%—mostly low- and middle-income African American women but also African American men and middle- and upper-income Whites—did the same. In Chester, where residents are less likely to own cars and have to travel to the suburbs for supermarkets, 96% reported choosing a supermarket as their primary food store. These figures follow national trends: the U.S. Department of Agriculture reports that 89% of households, regardless of income, use supermarkets or supercenters as primary food stores.

2. *Even in food deserts, people don't do most of their food shopping at corner or convenience stores.* This reality follows necessarily from the first point but deserves specific attention. Much of the popular discussion of food deserts assumes that people rely exclusively or primarily on locally owned corner stores or chain convenience stores. Yet researchers distinguish between food at home, including staples such as bread and milk, and food away from home, such as snacks, beverages, and restaurant meals consumed outside the home. In some neighborhoods corner stores might account for a substantial portion of food away from home, but they don't for most food at home purchases.

3. *Most people don't shop at the closest food store or supermarket.* Not only do low-income food shoppers skip over corner and convenience stores for food shopping, but they also frequently pass by a closer supermarket in favor of one farther from home. Across our studies, participants shop primarily at supermarkets more than a mile beyond the closest supermarket. This happens even when a new supermarket meant to address food deserts opens in an underserved area. Given that opening a supermarket is generally considered the major solution to food deserts, this is important to consider.

For numerous reasons, there is no guarantee that people will shop at a new supermarket: another supermarket is more convenient, prices or selections are perceived to be better elsewhere, and people are creatures of habit and continue their old shopping patterns. In our Chester study, 70% of participants shopped at the new store Fare & Square at least once, and 40% had shopped there four or more times in the store's first year. Proximity from home to the store was the biggest factor in how often they visited, but not everyone who lived nearby had shopped at Fare & Square, and not everybody who was shopping there lived nearby. Loyalty to a particular store and the quest for lower prices, better quality, or more culturally appropriate selection are explanatory factors. Sometimes choices are even driven by convenience, broadly defined as being near other places where people spend time—such as at work, in religious congregations, or with relatives—rather than just proximity to home.

4. *All supermarkets are not the same.* Variations on the traditional supermarket are increasingly common players in the food environment. Limited-assortment supermarkets, such as Trader Joe's and Aldi, offer fewer products, often at lower prices, because they require less retail space. Deep discounters, such as Save-a-Lot, Food 4 Less, and PriceRite, cater specifically to budget-conscious shoppers. Other more familiar retailers, such as Target and Walmart, have developed small-format stores with grocery options, following millennials back to urban centers and forcing the food retail industry to recalculate how to maximize sales in small spaces. Industry observers have their eyes on broader societal trends toward convenience and health consciousness, with expectations that grocery aisles reflect these shifts as retailers distinguish themselves in a crowded marketplace. Disruptive technologies, such as grocery delivery services and web purchases, stand to change the face of the brick-and-mortar food retailer. Thus, what we think of as the modern supermarket, wherever it is located, is subject to change. How shoppers with access constraints respond to these changes remains to be seen.

5. *Most people shop at multiple food stores.* Perhaps because supermarkets differ in terms of selection and pricing, low-income shoppers shop across multiple food stores, including meat stores, produce stores, farmers' markets, and other specialty retailers. In Chester, our study participants shopped at an average of more than four supermarkets a month.

6. *Most people drive or get a ride to do their food shopping.* In West Philadelphia, 70% of participants drive or get rides from a friend or relative; only 11% take public transportation despite Philadelphia's extensive public transportation system. Another 16% walk, and fewer than 2% ride a bicycle. Even among Chester respondents, who have a very low rate of car ownership, twice as many people drive or get a ride rather than take the bus to food shop. Another 13% walk, and 1% ride a bicycle. This reliance on driving to food shop—or at least for big shopping trips—is explained largely by the challenge, if not the impossibility, of carrying multiple bags of groceries on and off the bus, trolley, or train. For the relatively small group of people who rely on public transportation to shop for food,

proximity of transit stops is a significant consideration in choosing a supermarket.

7. *People shop at different types of stores for different types of food products.* In West Philadelphia, nearly half our participants reported shopping at farmers' markets, produce stores, and curbside fruit and vegetable trucks for produce. In Chester, where these types of produce outlets have been largely nonexistent, the main specialty food shopping trips are to meat shops. Wholesalers and big box stores provide a distinct set of food products, and trips to these generally complement, rather than replace, trips to conventional supermarkets. This reality is unremarkable until we consider the possible health implications. Further research is needed to understand health implications of shopping at limited assortment and deep-discount stores versus full-service supermarkets.

8. *Food safety, store cleanliness, and customer service really matter.* Low-income shoppers want the same experience that middle- and upper-income shoppers expect: fresh products that haven't expired, stores that look and smell clean, and staff who are helpful, pleasant, and efficient. The experience of shopping at local stores has taught low-income shoppers in Chester and Philadelphia not to expect the same kind of experience at corner stores, small grocery stores, and deep-discount supermarkets as full-service suburban supermarkets. These diminished expectations are a distinguishing feature of people living in food deserts.

9. *There is racial and economic sorting based on who shops where.* Food shopping reinforces economic and racial divisions in our society. Many food store choices are driven primarily by price; deep-discount stores may not offer a superior shopping experience, but food is generally less expensive there. In our study of moms participating in the WIC program in North Philadelphia, more than half reported doing most of their food shopping at a discount chain supermarket or local chain supermarket rather than a national chain. On the other hand, middle- and upper-income households are more likely to choose high-end supermarkets such as Whole Foods—10 times more likely in our West Philadelphia study. But income only explains part of this self-selection process. Black participants were

nearly 3 times as likely to shop at a discount supermarket as White participants, and participants without a college degree were more than 3 times as likely to shop at a discount supermarket as participants without a college degree.

10. *Outdoor advertising for tobacco and sugar-sweetened beverages is pervasive at small food stores in poor neighborhoods.* Health considerations relating to food stores go beyond the foods they sell. Many stores selling food also sell tobacco, and certain types of stores, including corner and chain convenience stores, are more likely to advertise tobacco inside and outside. In the absence of (now banned) tobacco billboards, corner stores are the new tobacco billboards, covered in poster-size ads especially in low-income neighborhoods. In a Philadelphia-wide study, we found that stores accepting (Supplemental Nutrition Assistance Program) SNAP and WIC benefits were significantly more likely to advertise tobacco inside and outside than stores not accepting SNAP and WIC. Stores selling tobacco and those advertising tobacco are significantly clustered in low-income neighborhoods. Availability of tobacco and the prevalence of tobacco advertising correlate with smoking rates.

Policy Considerations

According to the food desert model of policy, opening new supermarkets in underserved areas will decrease nutrition-related health disparities. Yet none of the changes that come with a new supermarket fundamentally change the cost of food or the delicate balancing act between paying for food and paying housing-related expenses. Low-income households might be able to save marginally on food shopping because of associated reduced transportation costs and lower food prices relative to smaller grocers. But food prices, particularly the price of more healthful foods such as produce, lean meats, and whole grains relative to less healthful foods such as sugar-sweetened beverages and processed foods, don't change. In fact, paying for food has gotten more difficult for many low-income households. Over the past two years, SNAP households have experienced reductions in

benefits totaling $8.6 million nationwide. We interviewed Chester
residents shortly after the reductions in SNAP benefits, which were
smaller in Pennsylvania than in other states. Heads of household
reported using a number of strategies to deal with the benefit reductions, including relying more heavily on food cupboards (29.9%),
relying more heavily on family and friends (15.6%), changing the
types of foods they purchase (13.0%), and reducing the size of meals
for adults (10.1%) and children (6.5%). These changes in behavior
occurred within a sample of households that were already experiencing food insecurity at a very high rate (85.5%).

Even under the best of circumstances, it is hard to imagine that
researchers will see reductions in obesity among people living near
new supermarkets without additional health-promoting interventions and increased SNAP benefits. Fresh food financing is neither
a silver bullet nor a bust but instead is somewhere in between, the
reality of urban food deserts—before and after they have new supermarkets—requires a new set of expectations for publicly subsidized
initiatives to improve access to healthful foods and decrease health
disparities.

To be successful, local, state, and federal policies to address food
deserts must recognize the following.

1. *Human health behaviors are complicated and don't change easily.* Even for well-resourced individuals, making and maintaining
health changes can be a struggle. This seems obvious, but if public
policies are rooted in an understanding of that, expectations about
changing health behaviors will be more realistic.

2. *Supermarkets, or the lack of supermarkets, is only part of the
problem.* Food environments in the United States promote overeat-
ing. These include restaurants, food stores across size and type, outdoor advertising, and other media. Supermarkets are only one part
of this food environment. Policies supporting new supermarkets
will have better health impacts if they are coordinated with policies
that address the broader food environment.

3. *All people deserve to make choices for themselves and their families.* Low-income households want what middle- and upper-income
households have: the ability to make choices. Policies that restrict

where people can redeem benefits such as SNAP and WIC or what foods they can buy with federal benefits deny people agency and control over important life decisions. An appropriate role for government is to ensure food safety and responsible food labeling and allow people to make safe and healthful decisions. The U.S. Department of Agriculture should continue to reject calls for restrictions on SNAP and WIC.

4. *Research is essential to understanding what works.* Policy efforts cannot always wait for definitive empirical evidence of their positive effect, but evaluation studies are critical and allow low-income households an opportunity to be heard. Research that identifies causal mechanisms between food environments, health behaviors, and health outcomes should be a priority.

5. *Government should invest in people and places.* New place-based resources such as a new supermarket are not useful if residents can't access them because of cuts in people-based resources. Cuts in SNAP benefits made no sense alongside increases in federal funding for the national Fresh Food Finance Initiative. In practice, people-based programs, such as SNAP, can have distinctly place-based effects.

6. *All communities should have a supermarket.* Just as urban residents expect clean air and water, good public schools, safe public parks, and well-maintained sidewalks, they should expect to have a supermarket within some reasonable distance, such as one mile. In places where private investment is lacking, local, state, and federal governments should assist with financing. This is no different than developers seeking a subsidy for a new hotel or stadium.

7. *Government needs to subsidize healthful foods for low-income households.* Helping finance supermarket development is part of that, but more direct subsidies for healthful food purchases such as pilot programs giving SNAP participants incentives for purchasing produce are needed to counteract long-term subsidies for foods, such as corn and soybeans, that have made many obesity-promoting foods so inexpensive.

8. *We need the support of the supermarket industry.* Some government regulations regarding advertising, in-store marketing, and

nutrition labeling can set standards, but it is unlikely that government can ever regulate end cap displays and in-store sales. We need
more retailers such as Jeff Brown, owner of several ShopRite stores
in Philadelphia and the poster child for fresh food financing, and
Philabundance, operators of Fare & Square in Chester, who have
a commitment to serving low-income communities extending
beyond profit. National players such as Walmart and Whole Foods
have shown some interest in increasing access to healthful foods
in low-income communities, but real change requires a long-term
commitment from a wide range of retailers.

9. *We need the support of the food industry.* No matter how pro-
gressive supermarket partners may be, they still must rely on food
manufacturers to stock their shelves. In particular, we need the support of the beverage industry and manufacturers of cereal and chips
to create and market more healthful products that taste good.

10. *Food is part of a broader spectrum of needs and interests.* Cities and low-income communities need coordinated urban policy to
deal with concentrated poverty. Food deserts cannot be understood
or completely eliminated without being connected to policies supporting living-wage jobs, affordable housing, and high-quality education for all. Food acquisition is fundamental to everyday life and
health.

Beyond issues of nutrition and chronic disease, the way we
acquire food relates to our broader sense of identity as consumers
and providers for our families as well as our sense of pride in our
community. As the people of Chester and Philadelphia have taught
us, food shopping and eating are integrated into the rest of our
lives—socially, culturally, and economically. Holistic thinking about
health and well-being that extend well beyond financing supermarkets is essential to addressing the challenges that have received significant attention as part of the food desert phenomenon.

Funding to support our research has come from the Robert Wood
Johnson Foundation (Healthy Eating Research 66953), the U.S.
Department of Agriculture (2010-85215-20659 USDI AFRI), the Rob-
ert Wood Johnson Foundation Health & Society Scholars Research

and Education Fund, the Center for Public Health Initiatives, and a National Science Foundation Graduate Research Fellowship. We are grateful to numerous colleagues with whom we have worked on research studies relating to food access. In addition to the coauthors listed in the publications below, we thank Shiriki Kumanyika, Latifah Griffin, Auguste Dutcher, Kaitlin Gravitt, Nicole Thomas, Elizabeth Wall, and numerous student and community research assistants for contributing to what we know about this topic.

Sources

Brinkley C., Chrisinger B., & Hillier A. (2013). Tradition of healthy food access in low-income neighborhoods: Price and variety of curbside produce vending compared to conventional retailers. *Journal of Agriculture, Food Systems, and Community Development, 4*(1), 155–70.

Cannuscio, C. C., Hillier, A., Karpyn, A., & Glanz, K. (2014). The social dynamics of food shopping in an urban environment. *Social Science Medicine, 122,* 13–20.

Cannuscio, C. C., Tappe, K., Hillier, A., Buttenheim, A. M., Karpyn, A., & Glanz, K. (2013). Urban food environments and residents' shopping behaviors. *American Journal of Preventive Medicine, 45*(5), 606–14.

Chrisinger, B. W. (2015). Reconsidering the Supplemental Nutrition Assistance Program as community development. *Journal of Nutrition Education and Behavior, 47*(3), 273–77.

Giang T., Karpyn A., Laurison H., Hillier A., & Perry, R. D. (2008). Pennsylvania's Fresh Food Financing Initiative. *Journal of Public Health Management and Practice, 14*(3), 272–79.

Hillier, A., Cannuscio, C., Karpyn, A., McLaughlin, J., Chilton, M., & Glanz, K. (2011). How far do low-income parents travel to shop for food? Empirical evidence from two urban neighborhoods. *Urban Geography, 32*(5), 712–29.

Hillier, A., Chilton, M., Zhao, Q., Szymkowiak, D., Coffman, R., & Mallya, G. (2015). Concentration of tobacco advertisements at SNAP and WIC Stores. *Preventing Chronic Disease, 12,* E15.

Hillier, A., McLaughlin, J., Cannuscio, C. C., Chilton, M., Krasny, S., & Karpyn, A. (2012). The impact of WIC food package changes on access to healthful foods in two low-income urban neighborhoods. *Journal of Nutrition Education and Behavior, 44*(3), 210–16.

Hillier, A., Smith, T. E., Cannuscio, C. C., Karpyn, A., & Glanz, K. (2015). A discrete choice approach to modeling food shopping behavior. *Environment and Planning B, 42*(2), 263–78.

Hirsch, J., & Hillier, A. (2013). Exploring the role of the food environment on food shopping patterns in Philadelphia, PA, USA: A semiquantitative comparison of two matched neighborhood groups. *International Journal of Environmental Research and Public Health, 10*(1), 295–313.

Karpyn, A., Tappe, K., Hillier, A., Cannuscio, C. C., Koprak J., & Glanz, K. (2014). Where urban residents shop for produce: Fruit and vegetable food shopping patterns and use of farmers' markets among low- to moderate-income households. *Journal of Agriculture, Food Systems and Community Development, 4*(4), 129–41.

Ulrich, V., Hillier, A., & DiSantis, K. I. (2015). The impact of a new nonprofit supermarket within an urban food desert on household food shopping. *Medical Research Archives, 3.*

CHAPTER 7

What Do *You* Do?

Ideas About Transforming "Work" in the United States

Roberta Rehner Iversen

Think about how many exchanges you've had at a conference or a party or in a casual meeting that go something like this:

"Hi, I'm Bobbie Iversen." "Nice to meet you. I'm Jamia X."

Maybe there will be a couple more polite comments. And then the inevitable comes: "What do *you* do?"

How many times have people asked you that question? How many times have you asked others the same? Very often, I'm sure.

In the United States your job, career, or employment pretty much defines you in the eyes of most. Holding a legitimate income-producing job—what is called paid work, wage work, or labor market work—is considered different from and more valuable than other kinds of work such as parenting, caring for family members, volunteering, or doing some form of artistic or political activity. In spite of the fact that these work activities are essential to a civil society, having paid work in the labor market is an unquestioned goal. Regardless of whether income is derived from an hourly wage or a salary, this goal is at the heart of what scholars call the work society, or a work-centered society.

So what's the problem? What's wrong with having your identity connected to your work, especially if we're encouraged to take pride in or find meaning in what we do for a living? The problem is that the work society's overemphasis on jobs in the labor market results in dire problems for workers and communities.

Overemphasis on Jobs Hurts Workers

One problem with the overemphasis on labor market jobs is that those with shorter life spans are replacing lifetime jobs. A related problem is that lower-paying positions in customer, retail, and fast-food services are dramatically replacing higher-paying positions in manufacturing and construction. For lower-earning less-skilled workers in particular, service jobs offer little opportunity for upward mobility. As the recent Great Recession graphically showed, too many workers hold precarious temporary jobs or no jobs at all.

Many workers experience harsh labor conditions. Workers who do keep factory jobs often endure dangerous labor conditions and are compelled to work extralong hours to increase productivity. Technological advances require many service workers to be available 24/7 and also be more vulnerable to exploitive practices. One example found in the course of my research is how an insurance company's customer service department in St. Louis, Missouri, provides too few workstations for its employees—on purpose. The shortage results in a "musical chairs" scenario such that when employees take a break they return to no seat. Because highly monitored service expectations are so great, loss of one's workstation, even for 15 minutes, subjects employees to inadequate productivity, income loss, and sometimes job loss. Also related, many big-box retail employees are subject to wildly varying work hours and schedules assigned with little advance notice. These practices make family budgeting and finding care for sick children particularly difficult. Equally concerning, too many youths ages 16 to 24 are unemployed today—over 2 million out of 20 million (more than 1 in 10) as of June 2016. Even earlier, the hiring rate for youths and young adults under age 30 dropped from 6.8 hires per 100 in 2006 to a low of 4.2 in 2009. In the work society, unemployed youths not pursuing postsecondary education have few legitimate earning opportunities because of an inadequate labor market.

Periods of unemployment compound these labor market and workplace problems due to inadequate or terminated social policy supports. Even seven years after the official end of the Great Recession, over 7 million former workers remain unemployed. More than 2 million of them have been without a job for 27 or more months, which makes them ineligible for unemployment compensation in all but two states—*if* they were even eligible for the unemployment insurance program to begin with.

In contrast, for those who are employed, minimum wage, fair wage, and living wage movements are important, to be sure, but they may not address safe working conditions, paid sick or vacation leave, and pensions or savings plans. These interrelated and growing problems for laborers in the work society fly in the face of America's long-held ethos of unlimited opportunity and economic mobility for all. Because most workers in the United States rely on earned income for their economic security, it is obvious that the majority of workers are financially vulnerable.

Overemphasis on Labor Market Jobs Hurts Communities

These dire problems affecting labor market workers also negatively impact communities. The shift to service-industry jobs and the parallel reductions in construction jobs have created devastating problems for the country's physical infrastructure. Women, men, and children are getting hurt or killed every day because of accidents caused by crumbling roads and bridges, derailed trains, inadequate airport runways, and disintegrating water and sewer pipes. Scientists give the United States a near-failing grade of D for woefully inadequate infrastructure improvement efforts.

The labor market also can negatively affect civic engagement. Civic and political organizations often do not have enough people to run or participate in them, which weakens vital aspects of a democracy such as voting, enabling older persons to remain in their homes, and transporting children to school. For example, trying to equalize student achievement through increasing parental involvement in schools is often thwarted because too many parents have to hold two or three jobs to make ends meet, which leaves no time to volunteer at school. Worse, volunteering for schools and civic organizations is often not seen as "real work" and does not command the status and social approval given labor market work. Yet civic engagement is critical to maintaining our democratic political system, our country's economic base, and our children's futures.

Finally, the overemphasis on labor market jobs results in treating such work as the primary solution to the social ills in the United States. We see this particularly in the welfare reform legislation of 1996, which requires most single mothers with children ages six or younger to go to work in exchange for financial assistance. Such assistance is also now temporary and limited to 60 months over a person's lifetime. Under the earlier welfare program, Aid to Families with Dependent Children, which was not temporary or lifetime limited, the value of supporting parents to care for their preschool children at home was paramount. By 1996, the value of labor market work replaced the value of child rearing, as signified by the current welfare program's name, Temporary Assistance for Needy Families. In the process, poor people performing important labor raising their children were cast as "lazy," "dependent," and requiring tutelage to develop a work ethic to receive minimal financial assistance to support their families.

What can be done to solve these individual and community problems caused by overemphasis on labor market work? Several solutions are possible, two of which I want to discuss here. The first is to transform how we do "work" and, particularly, how we do "paid work."

The second is to create policies and practices that make "doing work" possible for all.

Transforming How We Do "Work": The Postwork Society and Civil Labor

One way to address the challenges that individuals and communities experience in today's work society is to move toward what some call a postwork society. Given the provocative wording, let me begin by clarifying what a postwork society is not. Importantly, a postwork society does not mean ignoring constraining or dangerous work conditions, nor does it mean transforming into a leisure society. Postwork society simply involves *expanding* the idea of work far beyond the paid jobs in labor market organizations and businesses that we define today as "work." Postwork society means making more combinations of work and postwork possible by creating more varied pathways for income and meaningful activity, such as civic engagement. It involves broadening our vision for how we think about and reward work. Some put this even more strongly, seeing postwork society as "the call to refuse and transform the present system of work, rather than simply to reconsider or renegotiate a few of its terms and conditions" (Weeks, 2011, p. 101).

Transforming the work society into a postwork society then means (1) Rejecting the current work ethic posing labor market work as the highest calling and moral duty, (2) rejecting labor market work as the center of social life and the main way individuals access the rights and claims of citizenship, and (3) rejecting the privileging of labor market work over all other pursuits. ·

A more tangible vision for a postwork society involves labor market *and* civil labor, with *both* compensated. Civil labor includes engagement in the arts, culture, communities, and politics as well as parental labor, work with children, helping older or disabled persons, and responding to community needs. Civil laborers can participate in economic development, neighborhood beautification, and environmental and ecological improvements such as community gardens and much-needed infrastructure improvements. Regarding infrastructure, I was impressed decades ago when I saw vast cadres of men and women in Mexico City working on road improvements and neighborhood beautification. Although machines might have completed the work faster, Mexico obviously valued engaging human power over machine power to maximize paid employment and contribute to infrastructure improvements. Importantly, civil labor is not only community-focused and practical; it is socially recognized, valued, and rewarded with civic money, a currency we should utilize more in the United States.

Civic Money

The next question then becomes "How does civic money work?" Because civil labor is based in communities, civil labor can be funded in multiple ways, such as cash, exchange, and systems of credit. Having a variety of funding arrangements facilitates individualized civil labor patterns. Varied funding can also equalize people's opportunities to participate productively in *both* the labor market and civil labor. In this way, the idea of work moves away from the unachievable goal of a full employment society to the reachable goal of a multiactivity society (Beck, 2000, p. 36). In a multiactivity society, individuals participate in labor market *and* other forms of work, sometimes simultaneously, sometimes sequentially, and sometimes in one or the other or neither. As one example of a funding exchange process, in January 2015 a Philadelphia radio program reported on a community of artists in an economically disadvantaged part of the city whose space was paid for by a local funder. We know that space is critical for artists and that their work is often impossible without it. In exchange for this funding, for every hour the artists worked on their art, they were required to spend an hour on neighborhood community projects—especially arts and space-related projects but not exclusively. This hour-for-hour exchange exemplifies the transformative possibilities for lives and communities in a postwork society.

Not Enough Work Society Jobs

In reality, there aren't enough labor market jobs in the United States to go around. Here are the numbers. As of April 2016, about 324 million persons live in the country. Approximately 74 million are children age 17 and under, and approximately 48 million are age 65 or older. Subtracting these children and older persons from the 324 million leaves roughly 202 million persons who are of employment age, 18 to 64. However, only about 144 million of those 202 million are actually employed. At the same time, there are about 144 million jobs. This means that some 58 million people in the United States are doing work for which they are not paid—work that keeps society robust, communities strong, public schools effective, and civic organizations viable. Even if only half of these 58 million people want or are able to engage in some kind of paid work, 29 million people is a sizable and impressive pool of energy to tap for improving conditions. It is also likely that the figure would actually be higher, since many of the 5.8 million involuntary part-time workers would likely want to participate in civil labor in addition to labor market work. Senior economists also contend that during and after the recent Great Recession, another 2–3 million "marginally attached" and "discouraged" workers who left the labor market because they could not find a job would also come back if decent jobs—or, as I suggest, civil labor jobs—were available. This could increase the civil labor pool to around 38 million persons. That's a lot of person-power to "do work" in the postwork society!

Doing Work in the Postwork Society

Entrepreneurial and creative policies and practices facilitate doing work in the postwork society. One policy solution addressing the fact that there aren't enough jobs is the establishment of a guaranteed employment initiative. The community jobs programs of the New Deal and the current National Investment Employment Compact provide partial guides for a guaranteed job solution. Guarantees could easily move currently unemployed youths and adults alike into a postwork society, since both groups suffered severe unemployment and slow to nonexistent reemployment after the Great Recession. Guaranteed employment policy would need to be augmented by some form of universal basic income policy, perhaps one like Nobel economist Milton Friedman's earlier Negative Income Tax proposal but now available to all forms of work as well as to education, time-outs, family needs, and other so-called nonwork. Funding for such income proposals would likely reduce the amount of funds needed now for programs such as unemployment insurance, food assistance, and cash assistance. Funding might also come from the tax system in the form of income enhancements, such as the Earned Income Tax Credit, that today only pertain to labor market work.

At the same time, moving toward a postwork society does not erase the need to make labor market work conditions better, healthier, and more equitable. Some labor market work will always be needed. But this doesn't mean that labor market work is the only valid and valued kind of work possible. Trade unions and other civic organizations could as easily connect to civil labor as to labor market organizations, perhaps even easier.

A postwork society would likely be applauded by people in the younger generations, as has been found in Germany, and by the growing numbers of people of color in the United States—the groups often excluded from today's jobs. Equally troublesome for these groups is that the public-sector jobs that propelled many African American families into the middle class are now disappearing. Almost 2 million public-sector jobs—held by 1 in 5 African American workers—were lost during and since the Great Recession and have not been reinstated.

Doing work in a postwork society will also shift values. Even now, many in the United States express more inclusive, egalitarian values compared to those held by most in the work society, which we see in growing numbers of stay-at-home fathers and growing legalization of same-sex marriage. Postwork values are also visible in parents' calls to be able to split their time and energy for child rearing and income production in proportions that best suit their family. The answer to the question "How will people be economically sustained in the postwork society?" needs further development, to be sure, but creative entrepreneurial ideas have already been put forward in the United States and elsewhere, and more will come. As the earlier examples of artists in North Philadelphia and road workers in Mexico suggest, we might be surprised to learn how much of the postwork society is happening already. We urge the next president to increase the postwork society's pace and reach. This would be a win-win for individuals, communities, organizations, businesses, and governments alike.

Sources

Beck, U. (2000). *The brave new world of work*. Cambridge, UK: Polity.

Bernstein, J. (2015). Here's why wages aren't growing: The job market is not as tight as the unemployment rate says it is. *Washington Post*, January 12.

Bureau of Labor Statistics. (2016). The employment situation—June 2016. Washington, DC: U.S. Department of Labor, July 8.

Darity, W., Jr., & Hamilton, D. (2012). Bold policies for economic justice. *Review of Black Political Economy*, January 7 (online).

Department of Numbers. (2016). *U.S. employment and jobs*.

Domhoff, G. W. (2013). *Wealth, income, and power* (online).

Forsythe, E. (2015). *Young workers left behind: Hiring and the Great Recession*. Kalamazoo, MI: W. E. Upjohn Institute for Employment Research.

Garrett, P. M. (2014). Confronting the 'work society': New conceptual tools for social work. *British Journal of Social Work*, 44(7): 1682–99.

Gill, R., & Pratt, A. (2008). In the social factory? Immaterial labour, precariousness and cultural work. *Theory, Culture & Society*, 25(7–8), 1–30.

Iversen, R. R., & Armstrong, A. L. (2006). *Jobs aren't enough: Toward a new economic mobility for low-income families*. Philadelphia: Temple University Press.

Kalleberg, A. L.(2009). Precarious work, insecure workers: Employment relations in transition.2008 Presidential Address. *American Sociological Review*, 74(1), 1–22.

————. (2013). *Good jobs, bad jobs: The rise of polarized and precarious employment systems in the United States, 1970s to 2000s.* New York: Russell Sage Foundation.

Knowledge@Wharton. (2015, February 23). *The economy is coming back—why are wages stuck in a rut?*

Lambert, S. J., Fugiel, P. J., & Henly, J. R. (2014). *Precarious work schedules among early-career employees in the US: A national snapshot.*

Livingston, G. (2014). *Growing numbers of dads home with the kids: Biggest increase among those caring for family.* Washington, DC: Pew Research Center Social and Demographic Trends Project, June.

U.S. Census Bureau. n.d. *Baby boom generation to accelerate elderly and oldest old growth.*

U.S. Department of Labor. (2014). *Maximum potential weeks of UI benefits for new claimants.*

Weeks, K. (2011). *The problem with work: Feminism, Marxism, antiwork politics, and postwork imaginaries.* Durham, NC: Duke University Press.

Wessel, D. (2015). *Spending on our crumbling infrastructure.* Washington, DC: Brookings Institution.

CHAPTER 8

Forced Mental Health Treatment Will Not Prevent Violent Tragedies

Phyllis Solomon

In January 1999 Andrew Goldstein, a person diagnosed with schizophrenia and a long history of psychiatric hospitalizations, sent Kendra Webdale to her death when he pushed her in front of an oncoming subway train in New York City. On January 10, 2001, college sophomore Laura Wilcox was shot to death while working at a public mental health clinic during a school break by Scott Thorpe, a 41-year-old man who refused psychiatric treatment.

These horrific incidents outrage and scare the public, much of whom already believe that people with mental illnesses are violent predators. Although these events are extremely rare, they grab the media headlines for weeks, stoking fears regarding public safety and provoking responses from elected officials. Consequently, 44 states and the District of Columbia have passed assisted outpatient treatment (AOT) statutes enabling civil courts to mandate mental health treatment taking place in communities. In New York and California these laws have been named for their victims, Kendra's Law and Laura's Law, respectively. Currently there are two bills introduced in the U.S. Congress for mental health reform that both contain the expansion of court-mandated treatment. One is in the Senate,

S. 1945, Mental Health Reform Act, and the other in the House of Representatives, H.R. 2646, Helping Families in Crises Act. This is the first time in 50 years that major bills in Congress have dealt with issues of mental health. However, this expansion is unnecessary, as all states already have existing involuntary commitment laws allowing for psychiatric inpatient confinement for individuals with mental illness assessed to be *imminently dangerous* to themselves or others. While these laws may seem to be commonsense initiatives for preventing violent incidents, these AOT laws expand the policing power of the state and deny the civil rights of those not meeting the criteria for involuntary psychiatric hospitalization. There is much controversy and contention surrounding the ethics and effectiveness of AOT laws. This chapter delineates the reasons for opposing such laws and indicates why voluntary community treatment is more effective for achieving AOT goals of increasing adherence to prescribed treatment and reducing hospital readmission, homelessness, and involvement with the criminal justice system. These goals are good ones to have and are far more realizable with voluntary community treatment than initiatives seeking to prevent future violent tragedies.

What Is AOT?

AOT is a positive spin on coercive treatment. The term "assisted outpatient treatment" euphemistically coined by advocates of these laws to describe what for years has been called involuntary outpatient commitment, mandatory outpatient treatment, and compulsory treatment orders. Opponents call them "leash laws." Due to public fears regarding tragic incidents such as those that happened to Webdale and Wilcox, state legislators have been pressured to pass AOT laws. Civil courts can order people with severe psychiatric diagnoses, specifically those with schizophrenia, bipolar, and major depression disorders, into receiving forced treatment, usually involving prescribed psychiatric medication. In many states the authority to commit people with mental illness to outpatient treatment was already available through existing commitment laws; however, these legal mechanisms were infrequently used.

The provisions of these legislative acts vary from state to state. Essentially the laws apply to people with mental illnesses with a history of not adhering to prescribed medication. The presumption is that noncompliance in terms of treatment likely contributed to past hospitalizations, homelessness, incarceration, and acts or threats of violence. While this may seem like a fair assumption, these laws are expanding and blurring what constitutes dangerousness and, in the process, placing a range of people with mental illnesses under community surveillance. In some states these laws are applicable to those discharged from inpatient psychiatric services. In other states they apply to those with mental illness residing in the community who refuse voluntary community mental health treatment. When employed without prior hospitalization, the laws serve as preemptive measures for individuals with mental illness who are clinically determined to be deteriorating without psychiatric treatment intervention, usually prescribed medication. The use of the preemptive strike is based on the assumption that these individuals will likely meet criteria for involuntary inpatient treatment in the future. A civil judge issues the order based on the testimony of a clinically qualified professional, usually a psychiatrist.

It must be understood that outpatient commitment is not treatment per se. Some legislation, such as in New York, included funds for mental health treatment and services for the designated population falling within the jurisdiction of the law. When outpatient commitment provides services, it is referred to as a program. Whatever the case, community treatment is basically coerced.

The debate regarding coerced community treatment is not merely confined to the United States. It is also occurring in England, Australia, Wales, Scotland, and elsewhere. In England, these court-ordered mandates allowing for supervision outside the confines of hospital settings are referred to as community treatment orders. Ireland has not passed such legislation, as other mechanisms are available to achieve similar goals. In Ireland, as is the case in other places including the United States, individuals may be provisionally released from involuntary psychiatric hospitalization to the community. However, these individuals are provisionally or conditionally released as long as they comply with treatment orders. Technically they remain on the hospital census as inpatients and therefore can easily be returned to a hospital should anything go awry. This was a common practice in the past in the United States and remains the strategy in New Hampshire.

The Ineffectiveness of AOT

To date there have been only three studies from which can be drawn conclusions of effectiveness with regard to outpatient commitment. None have found support for a claim of effectiveness. There were no differences in continued service use, reductions in hospital readmissions, length of hospital stays, rates of arrest, rates of violent incidents, or improvement in social functioning for those under the commitment order compared to those on standard voluntary community treatment. The only positive outcome from these studies was that patients were less likely to be victims of crimes. It would require an inordinate number of individuals placed on outpatient commitment to achieve other positive outcomes such as reduced hospitalizations and arrests. Furthermore, even if these were minimally effective the impact on public safety would be negligible, given that only about 4% of violent incidents in the United States are committed by those who are mentally ill. In light of these findings, we can ask if there are more effective means than coercion to achieve the objective of treatment adherence. Are there not strategies for internalizing acceptance of treatment rather than using externalized coercion?

Proponents believe that these laws save states money. Again, this is a false claim. Studies show that by shifting costs from highly expensive inpatient treatment to community-based mental health services, savings can be accrued from reduced use of criminal justice services and less expensive mental health and medical treatments. However, the cost savings likely were not due to the law per se but more likely resulted from the receipt of more intensive services. Remember, the law is not about the use of services but instead is about the use of coercive orders to comply with treatment.

There are extensive administrative and legal costs involved in operating AOT, which inevitably varies by location and the degree of implementation. A study of New York City and five selected counties in New York State finds the average cost for the first 12-month period after hospital discharge was approximately $104,000 to $105,000 per patient, and in the second 12-month period after discharge the cost did significantly reduce but still remained extremely high, from $39,000 to $53,000 per patient. The final report to the New York State Office of Mental Health on Kendra's Law indicated that the operating costs for the fiscal year 2005–2006 budget were $32 million. In Summit County, Ohio, the per person cost were still $35,103 and then down to $17,540, and in this jurisdiction the patients were served within their existing outpatient mental health services. Furthermore, these costs likely do not include additional costs such as the police picking up noncompliant patients.

Overall, there are a host of questions raised by the evidence used to support these laws. Is it the coercive mechanism that produces these claimed positive results, or is the real potency coming from the use of needed intensive outpatient services? Therefore, is coercive treatment necessary or the most effective means to achieving the intended objectives of these laws? Are these legal mandates ethically justified to deny an already stigmatized population their rights to liberty and autonomy to make voluntary treatment decisions? Is the process by which these laws work morally and ethically right?

Enforcement of AOT Is Difficult and Costly

The investigators of the study of Kendra's Law stated a cautionary note regarding results being compromised, since no police orders to pick up noncompliant mandated individuals were issued during the course of the research. Therefore, there were no consequences for individuals noncompliant with treatment. Such situations are not unique to New York City but are the reality in terms of implementing such orders. Moreover, if the issuance of orders did not occur under the watchful eye of evaluators, it is unlikely to occur when unobserved. Providers do not want to spend time going to court, nor do they like being put in the position of police enforcer. Providers rightfully believe that attending court in these cases is a waste of time, as these individuals do not meet the criteria for involuntary inpatient admission. Similarly, police do not like to spend time picking up these individuals who are noncompliant, as they are usually only admitted to the hospital for a very short period of observation if at all. In two or three days at most the individual is back in the community. For these reasons, these laws have been described as having no teeth.

Providers do not like to work with involuntary clients. And frequently they don't know how to, as they are generally not trained to do so. Coercion in treatment can make the client resistant and undermine a therapeutic relationship, as there is an undercurrent of distrust. Client distrust makes it hard to establish or maintain a good working relationship with the provider. Without a relationship with a client, it is extremely difficult for providers to engage a client in services, thus defeating the intention of the legislation, which is essentially to coerce individuals who are nonadherent into treatment. This situation places providers in an untenable position.

Another aspect difficult to implement is the ability of clinicians to assess with any certainty who meets the criteria of these statutes. Research shows that clinicians' accuracy in assessing risk of dangerousness is notoriously poor. The assessment of risk for dangerousness criteria for inpatient commitment is much more circumscribed, resulting in greater accuracy of identifying the likelihood of a violent act being committed in the near future.

Opponents frequently label these statutes as forced drugging laws. However, these laws do not include forced medication. The treatment plan formulated by the judge can stipulate the taking of medication. But the question becomes how this stipulation is enforced. Direct observation may work up to a point in an inpatient treatment setting, as patients may still "cheek" the medication. But in a community setting it is far more complicated unless injectable medications are given. Moreover, a U.S. court of appeals established in *Rogers v. Okin* that a competent person has a right to refuse medication in nonemergency situations, even in a hospital or prison setting. Although proponents argue that patients under these orders are more compliant with prescribed medication, this adherence is usually inferred from receipt of prescriptions rather than observation of the drugs being taken. If patients under such orders are adherent to prescribed medication, it is usually due to threats of being returned to the hospital even if the provider knows that this is not likely in the immediate future. Their justification for this deception is that the client will deteriorate to the point of meeting involuntary commitment criteria. Thus, when these laws result in compliance, research has found that it usually involves deception on the part of the provider, which is an ethically questionable practice.

In jurisdictions where there is no operational guidance or administrative structure for implementing these legal mechanisms, they are unlikely to be implemented. In other locales in which structures are in place, there are undoubtedly high costs associated with them. It would seem that these funds would be better spent on voluntary mental health services than on administering such a program.

AOT Violates Civil Rights of Individuals with Mental Illness

When curtailing another's liberty and placing the individual under constant surveillance, there has to be a compelling argument to do so. These laws have the latitude of taking away autonomous decision making and rights to self-determination from an individual who has not been legally classified as incompetent or dangerous. The treatment orders stipulated by a judge may include where the individual lives and how the individual spends her or his days. Furthermore, the commitment orders are usually for a six-month period and can easily be renewed. There is a lack of clarity as to how many times they can be renewed, as there are no clear criteria for termination. This indeterminate sentence is extremely troubling and certainly a violation of one's inalienable right to liberty. This harks back to the old days when state hospitalization was indeterminate and some patients found the criminal justice system preferable, as a criminal sentence of incarceration and/or community supervision defined parameters, and when the sentence was over, it was over.

Proponents who take a liberty interest try to make the case that outpatient commitment is better than the alternative of confinement to a hospital or a jail or prison. However, these individuals have not met the standards for inpatient commitment and have not committed a crime. These are individuals with an illness who may benefit from treatment but have not been deemed incompetent or dangerous and therefore have a right to make their own treatment choices. Proponents further make the argument that since individuals are being served in the community and may otherwise be committed to a hospital, AOT meets the least restrictive alternative standard of the American with Disabilities Act as interpreted in the *Olmstead* decision. This federal court decision ruled that if a person could reside safely in the community with appropriate supports reasonably provided, then the individual should be served there rather than confined to an institution. However, this argument is a false dichotomy, as these individuals have not met the standards for inpatient commitment, nor have they broken any criminal law.

Other proponents make the argument that these individuals lack insight into their illness or are incompetent to make reasonable treatment decisions; consequently, others need to make decisions for them, which is seen as a moral justification to prevent further harm. This justification is the age-old paternalistic position pitted against patient autonomy that others know what is in the best interest of those with mental illness. This position is conceived as morally justified because a diagnosis of mental illness is too often misconstrued as the incapacity to make the best decision, which is usually translated as unwilling to take prescribed medication. However, individuals with a diagnosed mental illness, such as schizophrenia or bipolar disorder, are ipso facto considered incapable of making their own treatment decisions. But if an individual is so incapacitated, there are already legal remedies of guardianship laws in place, whereas lack of insight remains undefined with no definitive standards. In the absence of a legal determination of a lack of capacity to make treatment decisions, an argument based on possible future deterioration is not a compelling reason to deny an individual the right to treatment choice. Why such a stigmatizing law as outpatient commitment is needed is unconvincing, especially when there are other people with conditions who refuse treatment from which they could benefit including cancer patients, substance abusers, people with diabetes, and those who are obese, but these individuals are not coerced into treatment. However, no AOT laws have a prerequisite of a court-ordered capacity/competency hearing.

Another ethical issue involved in the implementation of these orders is the use of deception in patients mistakenly believing that there would be dire consequences if they are noncompliant with these commitment stipulations. In a recent study in the United Kingdom, providers were aware of these misconceptions but were unwilling to correct these false beliefs for fear that fully informing patients would undercut these orders. Moreover, these investigators found that the orders were most beneficial for those with insight into their illness and those accepting the authority of the practitioners but were "potentially counter-productive for those antagonized by it" (Stroud, Banks, & Dougherty, 2015, p. 89). It seems that those for whom this legal remediation is most targeted are not the ones who most benefit. AOT seems to work best for those who need it the least. The benefit derived from these legal mechanisms seems to be achieved through external forces, not from changing internal motivation to use prescribed medication in the absence of force.

AOT Further Stigmatizes Those
with Mental Illness

These laws have the inherent quality of labeling individuals to be at risk of violence. They are seen by some patients as "a threat to personal autonomy and their self-presentation" and a source of further stigmatization (Lally, 2013, p. 144). Furthermore, these laws perpetuate a belief in the dangerousness of those with mental illness. It seems acceptable to treat those with mental illness in this way but not those with other conditions who may benefit from coerced treatment. The moral argument is that it is a public safety issue. However, it further promotes negative views of this population as perpetrators of violence.

AOT Deters People with Mental Illness from Needed Treatment

Persons with mental illness, particularly with histories of hospitalization, fear that if they seek treatment from the community mental health system they may well be ensnared into these onerous commitment laws should they refuse prescribed medication. Individuals with mental illness frequently do want treatment but not necessarily drug treatment, with its aversive side effects and negative safety issues. Consequently, individuals who may need and could benefit from the services of the community mental health system find that avoidance is in their best interest. Such attitudes and consequent actions defeat the premises of AOT.

AOT Siphons Off Needed Services

Given that there are limited funds for mental health services, when providers are required to designate a priority to a specific group of individuals, the inevitable consequence is fewer services for others who may be equally in need. As a matter of fact, Andrew Goldstein, whose act of violence precipitated the passage of Kendra's Law, had sought mental health services on numerous occasions, only to be turned away. Ironically, had there been a Kendra's Law available to Goldstein, he likely would not have been eligible given his recognition and desire for treatment. A study conducted to provide information in consideration of Laura's Law noted that these laws essentially "commit" the mental health system to the provision of services to a designated group. While this is certainly a side benefit, it remains difficult for practitioners to assess and determine who falls under the purview of these laws. Moreover, these laws may function as an incentive for providers to place even more people on these orders so as to make them eligible for designated services. At the same time, the recognition by administrators that effectiveness of these laws is very much contingent on the extent of available community mental health services has discouraged some locations from implementing them.

Voluntary Treatment Is a More Effective Approach

When people feel that they have a choice in what services they receive and are involved in making treatment decisions, they are far more willing to seek treatment. Currently there is a new emphasis on patient-centered care in mental health, which is defined by the Institute of Medicine as "providing care that is respectful of and responsive to individual patient preferences, needs, and values, and ensuring that patient values guide all clinical decisions" (Institute of Medicine, 2001, p. 40). This approach, which translates into shared decision making, empowers patients, respects their dignity and worth, and invites them to collaboratively engage in treatment. The process of shared decision making has been shown to build trust, resulting in better outcomes for patients including being adherent to prescribed medication. This approach has been around for years in medicine but lags in mental health, particularly for those perceived as lacking insight into their illness—the focus of AOT.

Two psychiatrists, Drs. Mark Ragins and David Pollack, describe the success of employing this recovery-oriented approach with a patient with a long-term mental illness and a history of homelessness, whom many would say lacked insight into his illness and refused medication. The psychiatrist worked with the patient to determine what was important and meaningful to him. Collaboratively the client and the psychiatrist developed a plan to obtain the necessary resources and supports to meet the goals of obtaining housing and employment. With these in place and an established trusting relationship, the psychiatrist was able to address the need for medication. The patient was then willing to do so with the psychiatrist's explanation of how it may help him maintain his newly gained lifestyle. Recovery-oriented care gives voice and choice in treatment decisions rather them labeling a patient as resistant or noncompliant. This approach is far more successful in the long-term. As noted by a psychologist and consumer advocate, "psychiatric medications to support recovery . . . are not just medical decisions. They are also personal decisions that have a profound impact on individuals' lives" (Deegan, 2014, p. 487).

Conclusion

There is no compelling reason to pass outpatient commitment laws denying individuals with mental illness, who are determined to be neither incompetent nor dangerous, of their civil rights. Such laws are not effective in achieving their intended goals, likely defeat their intent of receipt of mental health services for those most in need, and in the process end up expanding surveillance in the name of treatment. What is needed is to provide more recovery-oriented community mental health services. AOT is not an effective means to compensate for an inadequately funded and poor-quality community mental health system. To deliver patient-centered care takes more time, effort, and skill on the part of practitioners. Consequently, more funds and training of providers are required, not forced treatment. The receipt of recovery-oriented voluntary mental health services is far more likely to pay off in the long-term rather than ineffective short-term solutions such as AOT.

Sources

Allen, M., & Smith, V. (2001). Opening Pandora's box: The practical and legal dangers of involuntary outpatient commitment. *Psychiatric Services, 52*(3), 312–16.

Burns, T., Rugkisa, J., Molodynski, A., Dawson, J., Yeeles, K.,Vazeques-Montes, M., Sinclair, J., & Priebe, S. (2013). Community treatment orders for patients with psychosis (OCTET): A randomized controlled trial. *Lancet, 381,* 1627–33.

Deegan, P. (2014). Shared decision making must be adopted, not adapted. *Psychiatric Services* 65(12), 1487.

Hamann, J., & Heres, S. (2014). Adapting shared decision making for individuals with severe mental illness. *Psychiatric Services, 65*(12), 1483–86.

Health Management Associates. (2015). *State and community considerations for demonstrating the cost effectiveness of AOT services: Final report.*

Heyman, M. (2001). Confusion about outpatient commitment. *Psychiatric Services, 52*(8), 1103.

Institute of Medicine, Committee on Quality of Health Care in America, Institute of Medicine. (2001). Crossing the quality chasm: A new health system for the 21st century. Washington, DC: National Academies Press.

Kisely, S., & Campbell, L. (2015). Compulsory community and involuntary outpatient treatment for people with severe mental disorders. *Schizophrenia Bulletin* (advance access).

Lally, J. (2013). Liberty or dignity: Community treatment orders and rights. *Irish Journal of Psychological Medicine, 30,* 141–49.

Matthias, M., Fukui, S., Kukla, M., Eliacin, J., Bonfils, K., Firman, R., Oles, S., Adams, E., Collins, L., & Salyers, M. (2014). Consumer and relationship factors associated with shared decision making in mental health consultations. *Psychiatric Services, 65*(12), 1488–91.

Monahan, J., Swartz, M., & Bonnie, R. (2003). Mandated treatment in the community for people with mental disorders. *Health Affairs, 33*(5), 28–38.

Player, C. (Forthcoming). Involuntary outpatient commitment: The limits of prevention. *Stanford Law & Policy Review, 26.*

Ragins, M., & Pollack, D. (2013). Recovery and community mental health. In K. Yeager, D. Cutler, D. Svendsen, & G. Sills (Eds.), *Modern community mental health: An interdisciplinary approach*, pp. 385–404. New York: Oxford University Press.

Rooney, R. (Ed.). (2009). *Strategies for work with involuntary clients* (2nd ed.). New York: Columbia University Press.

Steadman, H., Gounis, K., Dennis, D., Hopper, K., Roche, B., Stroud, J., Banks, L., & Doughty, K. (2015). Community treatment orders: Learning from experience of service users, practitioners and nearest relatives. *Journal of Mental Health* (early online).

Swanson, J., Van Dorn, R., Swartz, M., Robbins, P., Steadman, H., McGuire, T., & Monahan, J. (2013). The cost of assisted outpatient treatment: Can it save states money? *American Journal of Psychiatry, 170*(12), 1423–32.

Swartz, M., & Robbins, P. (2001). Assessing the New York City involuntary outpatient commitment pilot program. *Psychiatric Services, 52*(3), 330–36.

Swartz, M., Swanson, J., Wagner, H. R., Burns, B., Hiday, V., & Borum, R. (1999). Can involuntary outpatient commitment reduce hospital recidivism? Findings from a randomized trial with severely mentally ill individuals. *American Journal of Psychiatry, 156*(12), 1968–75.

CHAPTER 9

Beyond the Good Guy Versus Bad Guy Worldview

Improving the Gun Policy Debate

Susan B. Sorenson and David Hemenway

There are two types of people in the world,
those who divide the world into two types of
people, and those who don't.

—Robert Benchley

Dichotomous thinking. Sounds like a convoluted and complex process. But we use it all the time. Sometimes called black or white thinking, dichotomous thinking is a common, ordinary, and often helpful way to organize aspects of our reality. The tendency to think in opposites can be useful for quick decision making. But dichotomous thinking also has been linked with many negative psychological conditions. For example, it is common in borderline personality disorder and perfectionism. It has been associated with eating disorders and mood disorders, including depression and suicidal behavior.

Psychologists and psychiatrists are taught how to assess and treat dichotomous thinking. To change dichotomous thinking, a psychotherapist may point out examples and discuss different points of view in terms of a continuum in order to help patients develop more realistic perceptions of their environment and personal relationships. A problem with dichotomous thinking is that it keeps us in a childlike mind-set and unaware of all our possibilities.

Dichotomous thinking prevents us from considering possibilities at not only the personal level but also the societal level, thus limiting the perception of policy options. Although dichotomous thinking may be a good way for the leaders of single-issue lobbies to mobilize constituents to support or send money to the lobby, it is poor way to determine policy in a pluralistic society. As we discuss here, dichotomous thinking in policy is far too common in limiting the terms of what we know as the gun debate.

The phrase "gun debate" is an apt descriptor of discourse regarding gun policy. In debates, people take opposing sides and seek information supporting their positions. Gun policy debates often are restricted to dichotomous thinking, which promotes an "us versus them" mentality—gun owners versus nonowners, gun advocates versus gun grabbers, and so on. Dichotomous thinking classifies people as either progun or antigun and policy initiatives as either progun or attempts to take away guns from regular people. Dichotomous thinking can lead to futile debates over whether guns kill people versus people kill people, whether the real problem is gun availability versus bad individual behavior (e.g., mental health problems), and whether we should enact new laws or enforce old laws. Dichotomous thinking leads some to believe that if a law isn't scientifically proven to be effective it must not work at all or that a law is worthless if it doesn't solve every gun problem. Dichotomous thinking also leads to debate about whether we should use a criminal justice approach versus a public health approach to reduce crime and violence.

The most pernicious dichotomy in the gun policy debate is perhaps its assumption that the world can be neatly divided into good guys and bad guys. The gun lobby uses this framing to support its policy position that there should be virtually no firearm restrictions on the law-abiding "good guys" and harsh punishment for the criminal "bad guys."

Along with its deployment by lobbying groups, the good guy versus bad guy dichotomy has been a feature of high-profile survey research measuring attitudes toward gun policy. For example, a December 2014 survey by the Pew Research Center found that more Americans support gun rights than gun control. As it had for over 20 years, the survey presented the options as dichotomies. Media reports of such findings also reinforce the dichotomy, as if somehow one cannot support any restriction on firearms within the context of gun rights and vice versa. Simplifying the issue into two choices is misleading.

Unfortunately, for statistical convenience, models of gun policy often further a good guy versus bad guy mind-set. For example, in one statistical model "the population is divided into two groups: potential criminals and potential victims" (Mialon & Wiseman, 2005, p. 170). In another statistical model, the full benefit of having a gun is defined as reducing the probability of being assaulted, while the full cost is increasing the likelihood of suicides and gun accidents. These approaches are convenient, but they don't reflect reality.

A dichotomous mind-set is applied to gun accidents and suicides as well as interpersonal violence. Regarding suicide, the dichotomous mind-set claims that there are two types of suicide attempters—those who really want to die and those who don't. In reality, many suicides are spontaneous, and the desire to die is passing. Further evidence is found in more severe cases involving people hospitalized because of a suicide attempt: the overwhelming majority (over 90%) go on to die of the same things everyone else dies of, not suicide. Having purchased a handgun is associated with a remarkably elevated risk of suicide, a risk lasting for years. The risk spills over to other members of the household such that having a gun in the home is associated with a twofold to threefold likelihood of a suicide death.

These observations lead us to ask a patently offensive question: Are gun owners or people who live in households that contain a gun or guns more mentally unbalanced than others? (Notice the dichotomy in our question.) The answer, at least from what we know so far, is no. On some pretty basic measures of mental health, there is not much difference between those who do and who don't own a gun and between those who live with owners and nonowners. Gun owners and those who live with them are not more likely to have poorer general emotional and mental health, sadness and depression, or poor functional mental health or to have sought mental health treatment. Nor are they more likely to have thought about committing suicide or to have attempted suicide. They are just more likely to make a plan for suicide that involves a gun. Given that 80–90% of the suicide attempts with a gun result in death, those who use a gun in a suicide attempt aren't likely to get a second chance at life.

Some claim that gun accidents are caused by bad guys—criminals or self-destructive individuals—not regular people. Although one scholar claims that "about two-thirds of accidental gun deaths involving young children are not shots fired by other little kids but rather by adult males with criminal backgrounds" (Lott, 2013), data from the National Violent Death Reporting System say otherwise. In the accidental gun fatalities of children (ages 14 and younger), the shooter is also a child—even without including cases in which the child accidently shot himself.

Representative Thomas Massie (4th District, Kentucky), like some scholars and others, claimed that "Criminals by definition don't care about laws. They will get guns any way they can." He also stated that "Strict gun control laws do nothing but prevent good people from being able to protect themselves and their families in the event of a robbery, home invasion, or other crime" (Massie, 2014).

We believe that the claim that criminals, by definition, will not obey laws is bizarre. Although some people commit very violent crimes, this doesn't mean that they never obey any laws. Will they obey all gun laws? No. Will many be influenced by these laws and sometimes not obtain, carry, or use a gun? Yes. As researchers found nearly three decades ago, when incarcerated felons who didn't carry a weapon in the commission of their crimes were asked why, their answers indicated a law-abiding streak: 79% chose "get a stiffer sentence," and 59% chose "against the law."

A related problem with the good guy versus bad guy dichotomy is the tendency to emphasize blame rather than prevention. For intentional gun assaults this means blaming the shooter, with policy focused on punishing the criminal or disparaging the suicide victim. Notions of doing anything else to more effectively prevent gun assaults are classified as irresponsible and soft on crime.

In most other policy arenas, we have avoided such childlike dichotomies. For example, most motor vehicle deaths are caused by deliberate, unlawful behavior by motorists (e.g., speeding, driving drunk, texting, running red lights). As a society, we have been able to dramatically reduce motor vehicle deaths per mile driven not by changing driving behavior but instead by making cars safer (e.g., seat belts, air bags, collapsible steering columns) and roads safer. This does not mean that we were blaming cars and roads for our problems. Rather, policy makers were able to set aside claims that cars don't kill people, people kill people, and instead focus on how cars can be made safer. Similarly, we design subway systems, schools, and housing projects that are less conducive to violence without the irrelevant discussion of whether we are blaming the subway, school, or housing rather than the "bad guys."

With regard to violent interpersonal behavior, like most things in life, Americans fall on a continuum. On one end, there are clearly some extremely violent individuals from whom society needs protection. On the other end, there are nonviolent individuals who might serve as role models for the rest of us. But most people are far from perfect. For example, self-report studies indicate that most American males have committed felonies for which they could have been incarcerated, and a conviction for the felony would cause them to fail a firearms background check. Few bad guys are completely bad. And many improve over time; most convicted felons have stopped committing violent crimes by age 40—they age out of crime.

Given that there is no easy visible gulf between good and bad people, where, then, should gun policy draw the line for who is legally able to obtain, carry, and use a firearm? This is a crucial question for which we haven't had sufficient discussion. Should individuals with violent misdemeanor convictions be allowed to own and carry firearms? Should police chiefs whose officers have responded to multiple 911 calls to the home of an individual known to be violent have the discretion to deny him a concealed carry permit? A strong case can be made that as a society we have erred in drawing the line too close to the violent end for who can legally have a gun— and then made it too easy for those on the wrong side of the line to obtain firearms unlawfully.

For example, a study found that although the vast majority of homicide perpetrators in Chicago have long arrest records, most do not have felony *convictions*, meaning they probably could have passed a Brady background check. A recent study found that 60% of inmates in state prisons for gun offenses could have passed a National Instant Criminal Background Check System (NICS) check the moment before their most recent arrest. Most of the individuals in both studies were well known to the criminal justice system. What we know is that although there are some extremely violent individuals, most gun killings, especially if we include gun accidents and suicides as well as homicides, are done by those at more moderate risk. Even for gun homicides alone, the current cutoff for highest risk—a NICS background check—appears to miss most of the subsequent perpetrators.

We close our chapter with the words of the late Stephen Jay Gould:

> Among the devices that we use to impose order upon a complicated (but by no means unstructured) world, classification—or the division of items into categories based on perceived similarities—must rank as the most general and most pervasive of all. And no strategy of classification cuts deeper . . . than our propensity for division by two, or dichotomy. Some basic attributes of surrounding nature do exist as complementary pairings . . . so we might argue that dichotomization amounts to little more than good observation of the external world. But far more often than not, dichotomization leads to misleading or even dangerous oversimplification. People and beliefs are not either good or evil. . . . We seem so driven to division by two, even in clearly inappropriate circumstances, that I must agree with several schools of thought

... in viewing dichotomization more as an inherent mechanism of the brain's operation than as a valid perception of external reality. (Gould, 1997, pp. 55–56)

All the evidence, of course, indicates that the world is not bipolar but instead is continuous. Framing discussions of gun policy as good guys versus bad guys or us versus them ignores the available evidence and precludes the debate needed to develop policies to decrease gun violence. This chapter argues that the dichotomizations in the gun arena are truly dangerous oversimplifications, making it more difficult to reduce our gun-related problems.

Sources

Arntz, A., & ten Haaf, J. (2012). Social cognition in borderline personality disorder: Evidence for dichotomous thinking but no evidence for less complex attributions. *Behaviour Research and Therapy, 50*(11), 707–18.

Betz, M. E., Barber, C., & Miller, M. (2011). Suicidal behavior and firearm access: Results from the second injury control and risk survey. *Suicide and Life-Threatening Behavior, 41*(4), 384–91.

Bostwick, J. M., & Pankratz, V. S. (2000). Affective disorders and suicide risk: A reexamination. *American Journal of Psychiatry, 157*(12), 1925–32.

Byrne, S. M., Allen, K. L., Dove, E. R., Watt, F. J., & Nathan, P. R. (2008). The reliability and validity of the dichotomous thinking in eating disorders scale. *Eating Behaviors, 9*(2), 154–62.

Cook, P. J., & Leitzel, J. A. (1996). Letter to the editor. *Society, 33*(6), 6–7.

Cook, P. J., Ludwig, J., & Braga, A. A. (2005). Criminal records of homicide offenders. *Journal of the American Medical Association, 294*(5), 598–601.

Correa, H. (2001). An analytic approach to the study of gun control policies. *Socio-Economic Planning Sciences, 35*(4), 253–62.

Egan, S. J., Piek, J. P., Dyck, M. J., & Rees, C. S. (2007). The role of dichotomous thinking and rigidity in perfectionism. *Behaviour Research and Therapy, 45*(8), 1813–22.

Ellis, T. E., & Rutherford, B. (2008). Cognition and suicide: Two decades of progress. *International Journal of Cognitive Therapy, 1*(1), 47–68.

Gould, S. J. (1997). *Questioning the millennium: A rationalist's guide to a precisely arbitrary countdown.* New York: Crown Books.

Hemenway, D., Barber, C., & Miller, M. (2010). Unintentional firearm deaths: A comparison of other-inflicted and self-inflicted shootings. *Accident Analysis and Prevention, 42*(4), 1184–88.

Hemenway, D., & Hicks, J. G. (2015). May issue gun carrying laws and police discretion: Some evidence from Massachusetts. *Journal of Public Health Policy, 36*(3), 324–34.

Hirschi, T., and Gottfredson, M. (1983). Age and the explanation of crime. *American Journal of Sociology, 89*(3), 552–84.

Lethbridge, J., Watson, H. J., Egan, S. J., Street, H., & Nathan, P. R. (2001). The role of perfectionism, dichotomous thinking, shape and weight overvaluation, and conditional goal setting in eating disorders. *Eating Behaviors, 12*(3): 200–206.

Lott, J. (2013). Children and guns: The fear and the reality. *National Review Online*, May 13.

Mak, A. D. P., & Lam, L. C. W. (2013). Neurocognitive profiles of people with borderline personality disorder. *Current Opinion in Psychiatry, 26*(1), 90–96.

Massie, Thomas. (2014). Congressman Massie introduces amendment to restore the right to bear arms in the District of Columbia. Press release, July 16.

Mialon, H. M., & Wiseman, T. (2005). The impact of gun laws: A model of crime and self-defense. *Economic Letters, 88*(2), 170–75.

Miller, M., Azrael, D., & Hemenway, D. (2004). The epidemiology of case fatality rates for suicide in the Northeast. *Annals of Emergency Medicine, 43*(6), 723–30.

Miller, M., Barber, C., Azrael, D., Hemenway, D., & Molnar, B. E. (2009). Recent psychopathology, suicidal thoughts and suicide attempts in households with and without firearms: Findings from the National Comorbidity Study Replication. *Injury Prevention, 15*(3), 183–87.

Napolitano, L. A., & McKay, D. (2007). Dichotomous thinking in borderline personality disorder. *Cognitive Therapy and Research, 31*(6): 717–26.

Pew Research Center. (2014). *Growing public support for gun rights*, December 14.

Shafran, R., Cooper, Z., & Fairburn, C. G. (2002). Clinical perfectionism: A cognitive-behavioural analysis. *Behaviour Research and Therapy, 40*(7), 773–91.

Simon, T. R., Swann, A. C., Powell, K. E., Potter, L. B., Kresnow, M., & O'Carroll, P. W. (2001). Characteristics of impulsive suicide attempts and attempters. *Suicide and Life-Threatening Behavior, 32*(1), 49–59.

Sloan, J. H., Rivara, F. P., Reay, D. T., Ferris, J. J. A., & Kellermann, A. L. (1990). Firearm regulations and rates of suicide: A comparison of two metropolitan areas. *New England Journal of Medicine, 322*(6), 369–73.

Sorenson, S. B., & Vittes, K. A. (2008). Mental health and firearms in community-based surveys: Implications for suicide prevention. *Evaluation Review, 32*(4), 239–56.

Thornberry, T. P., & Krohn, M. D. (2000). The self-report method for measuring delinquency and crime. *Criminal Justice, 4,* 33–84.

Veen, G., & Arntz, A. (2000). Multidimensional dichotomous thinking characterizes borderline personality disorder. *Cognitive Therapy and Research, 24*(1), 23–45.

Vittes, K. A., Vernick, J. S., & Webster, D. W. (2013). Legal status and source of offenders' firearms in states with the least stringent criteria for gun ownership. *Injury Prevention, 19*(1), 26–31.

Wintemute, G. J., Parham, C. A., Beaumont, J. J., Wright, M., & Drake, C. (1999). Mortality among recent purchasers of handguns. *New England Journal of Medicine, 341*(21), 1583–89.

Wintemute, G. J., Wright, M. A., Drake, C. M., & Beaumont, J. J. (2001). Subsequent criminal activity among violent misdemeanants who seek to purchase handguns: Risk factors and effectiveness of denying handgun purchase. *Journal of the American Medical Association, 285*(8), 1019–26.

Wright, J. D., & Rossi, P. H. (1986). *Armed and considered dangerous: A survey of felons and their firearms.* Hawthorne, NY: de Gruyter.

CHAPTER 10

Child Welfare and Poverty

The American Paradox

Kara Finck, Debra Schilling Wolfe, Cindy W. Christian,
and Cynthia A. Connolly

America's successful future depends on raising generations of healthy, nurtured, resilient, and educated children. A robust and growing body of evidence documents that this future is threatened by problems that begin in early childhood and persist into adulthood. In the United States, children are presently the poorest segment of our society, placing us at the bottom of all developed nations with regard to child poverty rates. Correspondingly, almost 700,000 children each year are identified by child welfare agencies as victims of maltreatment. These problems are closely linked, and reducing child maltreatment will be most successful by addressing child poverty in a meaningful way.

Although the federal and state governments spend billions of dollars annually responding to child maltreatment, efforts have not addressed the most important predictor of maltreatment, namely child poverty. The United States addresses child and family health and social welfare-related issues in ways that differ from most of the world's industrialized nations. A series of political decisions and legislation over the course of the 20th century set the United States firmly on a fragmentary path that differed from most industrial societies, one in which children and their needs were viewed through the prism of social class. Policy makers assumed that middle- and upper-class children's needs would be met by their parents and that only poor children and families required governmental involvement in their health and well-being, an intervention that was purposefully stigmatized in an effort to disincentivize utilization of public welfare services.

In this chapter, we will review the impact of poverty and child maltreatment on adult health and well-being, explore the past and present barriers to intervention, and discuss failed and promising legal and policy interventions to address these problems.

The Formation of the American Model to Address Child Poverty

How the United States, one of the richest countries in the world, should help at-risk children has always been contentious. What kind of help, if any, should they and their families receive? Should assistance be paid for by the government, by private groups, or some combination of the two? Is the problem of poor children the fault of parental irresponsibility and immorality, or does it reside in structural frameworks within American social, cultural, political, and economic contexts? How should assistance, if any, be structured to avoid rewarding parental irresponsibility without hurting their children? (Katz, 2013; Davies, 1998).

Efforts to address these questions date back to the early republic and have almost always been politically contentious. For some, individual responsibility and limited government has long defined what it means to be an American; others disagree and have argued for a sturdy social safety net. As a result, there has been little enduring consensus on the best way to provide services, if any, to the indigent (Morone, 2004).

As such, reformers have historically sought to sidestep the questions above by focusing solely on children. The notion of aiding indigent adults is almost always grounded in distinguishing the "undeserving" (unwed mothers, for example) from the "deserving" (widows). There is consensus, however, that children are "innocent" and deserving of assistance and other opportunities to help them become model American workers and citizens. In other words, when it comes to providing a social safety net for children, Americans are less ambivalent than they are about helping adults, at least rhetorically.

For most of the 19th and early 20th centuries, children whose parents were too poor to care for them ended up in orphanages. Not only were these institutions highly stigmatized, but life for the children in the orphanages was regimented, often harsh, and child morbidity and mortality was high. A major federal conference convened to address the problem of "dependent" children in 1909 concluded that this practice was wrong. These reformers determined that the hundreds of thousands of institutionalized children with living, albeit indigent, parents deserved to live at home.

Their solution, publicly funded "mother's pensions," were adopted by some cities and states in the 1910s and 1920s. Providing a stipend to poor mothers so they did not need to place their children in orphanages became the template upon which the program Aid to Dependent Children (ADC) would be constructed in 1935. But unlike Social Security—an insurance program for all senior citizens—ADC families were scrutinized to make sure the mothers were "deserving."

The 1960s brought new attempts to address the problem of poor children in the context of the Great Society's war on poverty. That almost one-quarter of children were poor in 1964 was considered nothing short of a scandal in the richest nation in the world (Child Trends, 2015). While many new programs such as Medicaid and food stamps (later called the Supplemental Nutrition Assistance Program) were highly controversial out of fear that they would reduce adult incentives to work, those such as Project Head Start that brought services directly to poor children were less controversial because they sidestepped concerns about rewarding adults who had made poor choices and were thus "undeserving." Initiatives focusing on children attracted broad support across the political spectrum (U.S. Department of Health and Human Services, 2015).

A more conservative political climate in the 1980s and 1990s renewed debates about whether or not government had a role to play in solutions to poverty and even whether keeping poor children at home was in their best interests. In the early 1990s, for example, Newt Gingrich, Speaker of the House of Representatives, suggested in several widely reported interviews that society consider restoring orphanages to house indigent children whose parents were judged to be "bad" and "irresponsible" in order to break the generational cycle of poverty (Morganthau et al., 1994).

When President Bill Clinton signed the Personal Responsibility and Work Opportunity Reconciliation Act of 1996, the entitlement that had existed since the 1930s that guaranteed a stipend, however meager, to all extremely poor families ended. In the booming economy of the late 20th century and the first several years of the 21st century, child poverty declined. But since the 2008 economic downturn, it has since risen to virtually the same level it was when President Lyndon Johnson declared the war on poverty in 1964.

Amid an economic downturn in 2008 and 2009, poverty rates began to rise, and by 2014 child poverty was roughly the same (almost one in four children) that it had been when the war on poverty had been declared 50 years earlier (Jing, Ekono, & Skinner, 2015). And debates about poverty remained grounded in arguments of deserving versus undeserving, just as they have for more than 200 years (Bouie, 2014).

Today children are the poorest group, by age, in American society, and the youngest American children have the nation's highest poverty rates. Approximately 22% of all American children live in poverty, and an additional 22% live in low-income families (Jiang et al., 2015). One-quarter of American children under the age of three are poor, living in families whose incomes are less than the federal poverty threshold—$23,624 for a family of four with two children. From 1959 to 2012, estimated rates of childhood poverty declined from 27% to just over 22% (Council of Economic Advisers, 2014). In contrast, over the past half century federal programs such as Social Security and Medicare have successfully reduced poverty rates in senior citizens from approximately 35% to less than 10% (Wood, 2003). Moreover, among children there are great inequities in poverty rates by race and ethnicity. For example, more than one-third of African American and Hispanic children live below the federal poverty level, and approximately 44% of African American children under the age of five live in poverty (KIDS COUNT Data Center, 2015). Minority children are also more likely to experience chronic poverty, defined as poverty that lasts for more than five years (Magnuson & Votruba-Drzal, 2008).

Child poverty has profound implications for children's physical, intellectual, and emotional health in part because poverty is defined not only by economics but also by environmental and sociocultural influences that put children at risk. Poor children are more likely to live in households headed by single mothers who, in turn, are more likely to be victims of domestic violence, have higher rates of clinical depression, and struggle with substance abuse (Wood, 2003). Poor children frequently live in communities that have concentrated poverty, such as large urban cities. These neighborhoods often have failing schools, high rates of crime, less access to health care, and fewer social supports to mediate these problems.

Educational outcomes for children are also influenced by poverty. On average, poor children enter kindergarten less prepared for learning, have lower levels of reading and math skills, complete less schooling overall, work less, and ultimately earn less than their more affluent peers (Duncan & Magnuson, 2011). Poverty is associated with poor health outcomes throughout childhood. Infant mortality rates and low birth weight rates are notably higher in poor families and are influenced by race and ethnicity within poor communities (Sims, Sims, & Bruce, 2007). Poor children have higher rates of lead poisoning, higher childhood mortality rates, higher hospitalization rates, and a likelier diagnosis of severe, chronic health conditions (Bauman, Silver, & Stein, 2006). All of these factors influence the lifelong health of impoverished children in profound and lasting ways.

The Link Between Child Poverty and Child Maltreatment

Child maltreatment is a public health problem with lifelong health consequences for victims of abuse and neglect (Middlebrooks & Audage, 2008). Maltreated children have poor health, in part related to the associated risks of poverty, including parental substance abuse, mental health disease, and family violence and as a direct result of their abuse or neglect. Maltreated children receive less routine health care than their peers; they have high rates of growth abnormalities, untreated vision and dental problems, asthma, developmental delay, and early initiation of sexual intercourse; higher rates of sexually transmitted infections and early pregnancy; high rates of mental health disease; and a range of chronic medical diseases (Leslie et al., 2005; Simms, Dubowitz, & Szilagyi, 2000; Black et al., 2009; Carpenter et al., 2001; Boyer & Fine, 1992; Ahrens et al., 2010; McMillen et al., 2005).

Adult health outcomes for children who were maltreated are poor, and evidence confirms that early adverse childhood experiences such as maltreatment are the origins of many chronic adult diseases (Shonkoff, Boyce, & McEwen, 2009; Felitti et al., 1998). In other words, strong associations exist between cumulative traumatic childhood events such as maltreatment, family dysfunction and other social problems, and adult disease (Hillis et al., 2004; Edwards et al., 2003; Caspi et al., 2006; Schilling, Aseltine, & Gore, 2007; Gilbert et al., 2009). For example, rates of heart and liver disease, chronic obstructive pulmonary disease, autoimmune diseases, and sexually transmitted infections are higher in adults who experienced childhood adversity, including maltreatment (Dong et al., 2004; Dube et al., 2009; Dong et al., 2003; Anda et al., 2008; Hillis et al., 2000). Mental health disease and the use of psychotropic medications are higher in adults who experienced maltreatment as children (Horwitz et al., 2001; Anda et al., 2007).

The biological pathways by which child adversity affects adult health is an area of intense scientific investigation (Hillis et al., 2004). Evidence to date suggests that early childhood trauma including abuse and neglect can have profound effects on neurologic, hormonal, and immunologic systems that influence lifelong health. These data highlight the need for early childhood prevention of maltreatment, which is best addressed by looking at the root causes of maltreatment, including child poverty.

Poverty is one of the strongest and most consistent predictors of child maltreatment. In a study examining the effect of seven different variables on specific types of child maltreatment, only poverty and age of the mother were predictors of all types of child abuse and neglect (Lee & George, 1999). Numerous studies find that low socioeconomic status (SES) families have the highest rates of child abuse and neglect (Brown et al., 1998; Lauderdale, Valiunas, & Anderson, 1980; Gelles, 1989; Whipple & Webster-Stratton, 1991; Zuravin & Greif, 1989). Although child maltreatment is found in families at all income levels, there is a significantly higher level of child abuse and neglect of children living in homes classified as low SES. The U.S. Department of Health and Human Services found in its Fourth National Incidence Study of Child Abuse and Neglect that children living in homes with annual incomes of $15,000 or less were five times more likely to be at risk of child maltreatment than those with incomes of $30,000 or more. In examining type of abuse, the risk was three times as great for physical abuse and seven times as great for neglect (Sedlak et al., 2010).

A variety of studies have examined the relationship between income and maltreatment rates at the state, county, and neighborhood levels. Higher incidence of child maltreatment exists in those states with higher proportions of very poor children, higher levels of unemployment, and larger proportions of working single mothers (Paxson & Waldfogel, 1999, 2002, 2003). County-level research indicates that higher income inequality equates with higher incidence of child maltreatment (Eckenrode et al., 2014). And in a review of 25 different studies that assessed the influence of geographically defined neighborhoods, neighborhood structural factors, particularly economic, are most consistently correlated with child maltreatment (Coulton et al., 2007).

These data all support the current argument that there are indeed higher rates of child maltreatment among poor families (Straus & Gelles, 1986; Pelton, 1978; Drake & Jonson-Reid, 2014). And although recent studies have identified reporting biases that result in lower SES families being reported for suspected child maltreatment more frequently than their middle-class counterparts, it is likely that abuse does occur more often among lower SES families. It is unclear, however, whether this relationship is causal or simply a correlation. Multiple factors contribute to the connection between poverty and child abuse and neglect (Berger, 2004). For example, Waldfogel identifies four theories about the relationship between child maltreatment and poverty:

The stress associated with low-income status results in maltreatment;

Poor families are not at increased risk of hurting their children but are just more likely to be reported for child abuse;

Families who are poor are reported for neglect more often because they can't provide for their children; and

An underlying factor is influencing the correlation between poverty and neglect. (Waldfogel, 2001)

The correlation between poverty and child maltreatment is likely the result of a number of factors. For example, families who seek public services come before mandated reporters more often, may be scrutinized more closely, and can be subjected to different assumptions than their higher SES counterparts. Children often are reported as victims of neglect as a *result* of poverty. The quality of and access to services for families without financial resources can also place children at greater risk. The complexity of this issue points to a myriad of compounding factors resulting in the correlation between poverty and child maltreatment.

Legal Responses to Child Maltreatment and Poverty

In light of the demonstrable link between child maltreatment and poverty, you would anticipate that the legal response to child abuse and neglect incorporates an assessment of the impact of poverty on family safety and legislative reform focuses on the efficacy of anti-poverty programs on reducing the incidence of child abuse and neglect. However, child welfare laws have been historically silent on the link between child maltreatment and poverty. Furthermore, legislative reform and funding have focused on permanency and time-lines once a child is in foster care as opposed to preventive strategies providing tangible supports to impoverished families.

Laws regarding child abuse and neglect reach far and wide and differ by state in terms of determining what constitutes abuse and neglect, under what circumstances a child can be placed in foster care, and how long a child can remain in the state's custody. Historically, this has meant a range of legal responses for addressing child maltreatment and improving outcomes for children in the child welfare system. For example, youth can stay in foster care until they are 21 years old in Pennsylvania and California, but the requirements for remaining eligible for care differ in each of the jurisdictions (National Resource Center on Youth Development, 2013). Furthermore, some states don't permit young people to remain in care after they turn 18 or 19, allowing them to age out of the system whether or not they have economic or social stability at the time (N.M. Stat § 32A-1.8).

Similarly, there is no consensus as to whether the law should specifically exempt poverty as a legal ground for determining in court that a child is neglected and therefore able to be placed in foster care or that parental rights should be terminated. Indeed, only a few jurisdictions explicitly exempt poverty as legal grounds for neglect. In New York, the definition of a neglected child specifies that a parent's failure to provide food, clothing, shelter, or education must be assessed in terms of their financial ability or if they were offered "financial or other reasonable means to do so" (N.Y. Fam. Crt. Act § 1012 [f] [A]). In the District of Columbia, the law states that "the deprivation is not due to the lack of financial means of his or her parent, guardian, or custodian" (D.C. Code §16-2301 [9][a] [ii]). Connecticut's definition specifies that the grounds for neglect must be "for reasons other than being impoverished" (Conn. Gen. Stat. § 46b-120). In addition, courts have long noted that poverty may not be the only evidence provided to sustain a finding of abuse or neglect against a parent (*In re* D.S., 88 A.3d 678 [D.C. 2014]). As many have noted, poverty is never explicitly stated as the reason for child maltreatment but instead is defined as neglect in case law because of a failure to supply adequate food, housing, or medical care (Duva & Metzger, 2010). As Professor Martin Guggenheim noted, "it is rather that but for being poor, there would never be a prosecution" (Duva & Metzger, 2010, p. 63). Others have noted that the compendium of factors used by courts to make findings of abuse or neglect or in more extreme circumstances to terminate parental rights are directly related to parental poverty, including persistent unemployment, homelessness or inadequate housing, and chronic food instability.

The impact of explicitly distinguishing poverty and child maltreatment should not be underestimated. The vast majority of cases brought to the attention of child welfare agencies and ultimately adjudicated by courts concern neglect issues. By implicitly recognizing the link, child welfare agencies and by default courts are forced to assess factors related to poverty and expand their notion of a family's needs and appropriate responses. In part, the system could begin a subtle but powerful shift toward engaging families in preventive services aimed at reducing poverty, such as income supports and access to subsidized child care. This would be a dramatic change from the traditional model of service delivery to parents and children focused primarily on parenting skills, counseling, and substance abuse treatment. The traditional model's focus on engagement or compliance with services does not address needs related to poverty that would be better met through a focus on targeted resources and tangible supports such as nutrition, home visiting, and early intervention. However, the legal response must be one that is nationally focused to prevent the patchwork of reforms and policies that currently define the child welfare system.

Promising Programs and Policies

In order to understand the potential impact of antipoverty programs on child maltreatment, we must first put into context the amount of resources designated for child maltreatment. In addition to the long-term impact of child maltreatment on health and well-being (Sedlak et al., 2010), the financial costs associated with child abuse and neglect are astronomical. The lifetime cost for just one year of substantiated child abuse and neglect cases is estimated at $124 billion. In 2010, each case of nonfatal child abuse incurred lifetime costs of $210,012, including $32,648 in childhood health care costs, $10,530 in adult medical costs, $7,728 in child welfare costs, $6,747 in criminal justice costs, $7,999 in special education costs, and $144,360 in productivity losses. For cases of child maltreatment fatalities, the estimated average lifetime cost per death is $1,272,900, including $14,100 in medical costs and $1,258,800 in productivity losses (Fang et al., 2012).

The costs, of course, are not isolated. Scholars have noted the overwhelmingly poor outcomes on a number of social, well-being, and economic metrics particularly for young people who age out of the foster care system without being adopted or reunified with their families. For those young people who are exiting in some states at age 18, the likelihood of ending up homeless, without a college education or stable employment is higher. However, recent legislative efforts to allow state to extend jurisdiction until foster youths are 21 years old may have the potential to impact educational outcomes, as one example. Researchers have noted that "allowing foster youth to remain in care until age twenty-one could lead to a significant increase in educational attainment, which in turn would result in significantly higher lifetime earnings" (Dworsky, Courtney, & Pollack, 2009).

The costs experienced by older foster youths include poor heath, financial instability, and homelessness, among others detailed earlier in this chapter. Critically, though, those costs also implicate broader social and economic costs (Waldfogel, 2010). In sum, the short- and long-term costs are significant, and there is reason to believe that a concerted effort to reduce child poverty would have a collateral effect on the rates of child maltreatment and consequent involvement in the foster care system.

One model for addressing child poverty in order to reduce child maltreatment can be found in Britain's successful efforts to cut child poverty in half. In 1999 Prime Minister Tony Blair pledged to erase child poverty, and over a 10-year period the government succeeded in reducing the rate of child poverty by more than half. The reforms included programs aimed at increasing adult employment, providing additional financial supports for families, and increasing funding in children's programs. Researchers have noted the important lessons that could be imported into an American regime to reduce child poverty and collaterally decrease the rates of child maltreatment as a result (Waldfogel, 2010). Researchers have already demonstrated increased spending by low-income families on children's clothing, toys, and books in addition to improved well-being and health outcomes for young children and adolescents as a result of the antipoverty initiatives. This suggests that there can be an impact not only on the rates of child poverty but also on the rates of child maltreatment (Gregg, Waldfogel, & Washbrook, 2005; NESS Research Team, 2008). Ongoing research will hopefully shed light on the extent of the impact on both child maltreatment and long-term health and well-being. However, what is clear now is that the program was successful in reducing the rate of poverty in children because it set an ambitious goal and provided continued financial support in the form of services to children, incentives for parents to work, and additional financial support for families. Researchers estimate that similar investments in the United States would have been around $150 billion in 2008, almost half of what is spent on the

Earned Income Tax Credit, the Supplemental Nutrition Assistance Program, child care, and Temporary Assistance for Needy Families combined (Smeeding & Waldfogel, 2010).

Children remain popular on both sides of the aisle. No candidate was ever elected on an overt antichildren platform, and we propose learning from history. Rather than trying to seek consensus on the "why" of poverty, we suggest a solution that is framed in market pragmatism. Rather than providing services to poor children because it is the right thing to do, we draw on new research in brain science and economics that suggests a solution that will save money in the long term. Ultimately, we argue that impacting child maltreatment in any significant way means fostering policies and legislation that reduce poverty for both children and adults. We make this argument while remaining morally neutral about the American tradition of labeling certain adults "deserving" or "undeserving." Rather, we stipulate that since having an impoverished parent puts a child at increased risk, providing health care, educational support, child care, nutritional support, and other assistance ultimately benefits the next generation of Americans (Heckman, 2015). If the political will exists to set an ambitious goal of decreasing child poverty, then the corresponding fiscal investment must be sustained and targeted at improving living standards. As Jane Waldfogel notes, "if Britain could cut absolute child poverty in half in ten years, the US, and other wealthy nations, can too" (Waldfogel, 2010).

The authors would like to thank Sarah Wasch, MSW, for her assistance in editing this chapter.

Sources

Ahrens, K. R., Richardson, L. P., Courtney, M. E., McCarty, C., Simoni, J., & Katon, W. (2010). Laboratory-diagnosed sexually transmitted infections in former foster youth compared with peers. *Pediatrics, 126*(1), e97–e103.

Anda, R. F., Brown, D. W., Dube, S. R., Bremner, J. D., Felitti, V. J., & Giles, W. H. (2008). Adverse childhood experiences and chronic obstructive pulmonary disease in adults. *American Journal of Preventive Medicine,* *34*(5), 396–403.

Anda, R. F., Brown, D. W., Felitti, V. J., Bremner, J. D., Dube, S. R., & Giles, W. H. (2007). Adverse childhood experiences and prescribed psychotropic medications in adults. *American Journal of Preventive Medicine 32*(5), 389–94.

Bauman, L. J., Silver, E. J., & Stein, R. E. (2006). Cumulative social disadvantage and child health. *Pediatrics, 117*(4), 1321–28.

Berger, L. M. (2004). Income, family structure, and child maltreatment risk. *Children and Youth Services Review, 26*(8), 725–48.

Black, M. M., Oberlander, S. E., Lewis, T., Knight, E. D., Zolotor, A. J., Litrownik, A. J., Thompson, R., Dubowitz, H., & English, D. E. (2009). Sexual intercourse among adolescents maltreated before age 12: A prospective investigation. *Pediatrics, 124*(3), 941–49.

Bouie, J. (2014). What Paul Ryan gets wrong about "inner-city" poverty. *Daily Beast,* March 12.

Boyer, D., & Fine, D. (1992). Sexual abuse as a factor in adolescent pregnancy and child maltreatment. *Family planning perspectives,* 4–19.

Brown, J., Cohen, P., Johnson, J. G., & Salzinger, S. (1998). A longitudinal analysis of risk factors for child maltreatment: Findings of a 17-year prospective study of officially recorded and self-reported child abuse and neglect. *Child Abuse & Neglect, 22*(11), 1065–78.

Carpenter, S. C., Clyman, R. B., Davidson, A. J., & Steiner, J. F. (2001). The association of foster care or kinship care with adolescent sexual behavior and first pregnancy. *Pediatrics, 108*(3), e46.

Caspi, A., Harrington, H., Moffitt, T. E., Milne, B. J., & Poulton, R. (2006). Socially isolated children 20 years later: Risk of cardiovascular disease. *Archives of Pediatrics & Adolescent Medicine, 160*(8), 805–11.

Child Trends (2015). War on poverty. Retrieved from www.childtrends.org /our-research/poverty/war-on-poverty/

Conn. Gen. Stat. § 46b-120.

Coulton, C. J., Crampton, D. S., Irwin, M., Spilsbury, J. C., & Korbin, J. E. (2007). How neighborhoods influence child maltreatment: A review of the literature and alternative pathways. *Child abuse & neglect, 31*(11), 1117–42.

Council of Economic Advisers. (2014). *The war on poverty 50 years later: A Progress report.* Retrieved from https://www.whitehouse.gov/sites/default /files/docs/50th_anniversary_cea_report_-_final_post_embargo.pdf

Davies, G. (1998). *Linda Gordon, pitied but not entitled: Single mothers and the history of welfare* (New York: Free Press, 1994).

D.C. Code §16-2301 (9)(a)(ii).

Dong, M., Dube, S. R., Felitti, V. J., Giles, W. H., & Anda, R. F. (2003). Adverse childhood experiences and self-reported liver disease: New insights into the causal pathway. *Archives of Internal Medicine, 163*(16), 1949–56.

Dong, M., Giles, W. H., Felitti, V. J., Dube, S. R., Williams, J. E., Chapman, D. P., & Anda, R. F. (2004). Insights into causal pathways for ischemic heart disease adverse childhood experiences study. *Circulation, 110*(13), 1761–66.

Drake, B., & Jonson-Reid, M. (2014). Poverty and child maltreatment. In J. E. Korbin & R. D. Krugman (Eds.). *Handbook of Child Maltreatment.* Springer Science + Business Media.

Dube, S. R., Fairweather, D., Pearson, W. S., Felitti, V. J., Anda, R. F., & Croft, J. B. (2009). Cumulative childhood stress and autoimmune diseases in adults. *Psychosomatic Medicine, 71*(2), 243–50.

Duncan, G. J., & Magnuson, K. (2011). The long reach of early childhood poverty. *Pathways* (Winter), 22–27.

Duva, J., & Metzger, S. (2010). Addressing poverty as a major risk factor in child neglect: Promising policy and practice. *Protecting Children 25*(1), 63–74.

Dworsky, A., Courtney, M. E., & Pollack, H. (2009). *Extending foster care to age 21: Weighing the costs to government against the benefits to youth.* Chicago: Chapin Hall at the University of Chicago.

Eckenrode, J., Smith, E. G., McCarthy, M. E., & Dineen, M. (2014). Income inequality and child maltreatment in the United States. *Pediatrics, 133*(3), 454–61.

Edwards, V. J., Holden, G. W., Felitti, V. J., & Anda, R. F. (2003). Relationship between multiple forms of childhood maltreatment and adult mental health in community respondents: Results from the adverse childhood experiences study. *American Journal of Psychiatry, 160*(8), 1453–60.

Fang, X., Brown, D. S., Florence, C. S., & Mercy, J. A. (2012). The economic burden of child maltreatment in the United States and implications for prevention. *Child Abuse & Neglect, 36*(2), 156–65.

Felitti, V. J., Anda, R. F., Nordenberg, D., Williamson, D. F., Spitz, A. M., Edwards, V., Koss, M. P., & Marks, J. S. (1998). Relationship of childhood abuse and household dysfunction to many of the leading causes of death in adults: The Adverse Childhood Experiences (ACE) Study. *American Journal of Preventive medicine, 14*(4), 245–58.

Gelles, R. J. (1989). Child abuse and violence in single-parent families: Parent absence and economic deprivation. *American Journal of Orthopsychiatry, 59*(4), 492.

Gilbert, R., Widom, C. S., Browne, K., Fergusson, D., Webb, E., & Janson, S. (2009). Burden and consequences of child maltreatment in high-income countries. *The Lancet, 373*(9657), 68–81.

Gregg, P., Waldfogel, J., & Washbrook, E. (2005). That's the way the money goes: Expenditure patterns as real incomes rise for the poorest families with children. *A More Equal Society*, 251–76.

Heckman, J. (2015). The Heckman Equation. http://heckmanequation.org/

Hillis, S. D., Anda, R. F., Dube, S. R., Felitti, V. J., Marchbanks, P. A., & Marks, J. S. (2004). The association between adverse childhood experiences and adolescent pregnancy, long-term psychosocial consequences, and fetal death. *Pediatrics, 113*(2), 320–27.

Hillis, S. D., Anda, R. F., Felitti, V. J., Nordenberg, D., & Marchbanks, P. A. (2000). Adverse childhood experiences and sexually transmitted diseases in men and women: A retrospective study. *Pediatrics, 106*(1), e11.

Horwitz, A. V., Widom, C. S., McLaughlin, J., & White, H. R. (2001). The impact of childhood abuse and neglect on adult mental health: A prospective study. *Journal of Health and Social Behavior*, 184–201.

In re D.S., 88 A.3d 678 (D.C. 2014).

Jiang, Y., Ekono, M., & Skinner, C. (2015). *Basic facts about low-income children: Children 6 through 11 years, 2013*. New York: National Center for Children in Poverty, Mailman School of Public Health, Columbia University.

Katz, M. B. (2013). *The undeserving poor: America's enduring confrontation with poverty* (fully updated and revised ed.). New York: Oxford University Press.

KIDS COUNT Data Center. (2015). Children in poverty (100%) by age group and race and ethnicity. Retrieved from http://datacenter.kidscount.org/data/tables/8447-children-in-poverty-100-by-age-group-and-race-and-ethnicity?loc=1&loct=1#detailed/1/any/false/36/2664,2322,3654,2757,4087,3307,3301|/17079,17080

Lauderdale, M., Valiunas, A., & Anderson, R. (1980). Race, ethnicity, and child maltreatment: An empirical analysis. *Child Abuse & Neglect, 4*(3), 163–69.

Lee, B. J., & George, R. M. (1999). Poverty, early childbearing, and child maltreatment: A multinomial analysis, *Children and Youth Services Review, 21*(9–10) (September–October), 755–80.

Leslie, L. K., Gordon, J. N., Meneken, L., Premji, K., Michelmore, K. L., & Ganger, W. (2005). The physical, developmental, and mental health needs of young children in child welfare by initial placement type. *Journal of Developmental and Behavioral Pediatrics, 26*(3), 177–85.

Magnuson K. A., & Votruba-Drzal, E. (2008). *Enduring influences of child-hood poverty.* Madison: University of Wisconsin–Madison, Institute for Research on Poverty.

McMillen, J. C., Zima, B. T., Scott, L. D., Auslander, W. F., Munson, M. R., Ollie, M. T., & Spitznagel, E. L. (2005). Prevalence of psychiatric disorders among older youths in the foster care system. *Journal of the American Academy of Child & Adolescent Psychiatry, 44*(1), 88–95.

Middlebrooks, J. S., & Audage, N. C. (2008). *The effects of childhood stress on health across the lifespan.* Project Report. National Center for Injury Prevention and Control of the Centers for Disease Control and Prevention.

Morganthau, T., Springen, K. Smith, V. E., Rosenberg, D., Beals, G., Bogert, C., Gegax, T. T., & Joseph, N. (1994, December 12). The orphanage. *Newsweek,* 28–32.

Morone, J. A. (2004). *Hellfire nation: The politics of sin in American history.* New Haven, CT: Yale University Press.

National Resource Center on Youth Development (2013). State Pages, http://www.nrcyd.ou.edu/state-pages/state/ca and http://www.nrcyd.ou.edu/state-pages/state?state=pa

NESS Research Team. (2008). *The impact of Sure Start Local Programmes on three year olds and their families.* London: DCSF.

N.M. Stat § 32A-1.8.

N.Y. Fam. Crt. Act § 1012 (f) (A).

Paxson, C., & Waldfogel, J. (1999). Parental resources and child abuse and neglect. *American Economic Review,* 239–44.

———. (2002). Work, welfare, and child maltreatment. *Journal of Labor Economics, 20*(3), 435–74.

———. (2003). Welfare reforms, family resources, and child maltreatment. *Journal of Policy Analysis and Management, 22*(1), 85–113.

Pelton, L. H. (1978). Child abuse and neglect: The myth of classlessness. *American Journal of Orthopsychiatry, 48*(4), 608–17.

Schilling, E. A., Aseltine, R. H., & Gore, S. (2007). Adverse childhood experiences and mental health in young adults: A longitudinal survey. *BMC Public Health 7*(1), 30–40.

Sedlak, A. J., Mettenburg, J., Basena, M., Peta, I., McPherson, K., & Greene, A. (2010). *Fourth national incidence study of child abuse and neglect (NIS-4).* Washington, DC: U.S. Department of Health and Human Services.

Shonkoff, J. P., Boyce, W. T., & McEwen, B. S. (2009). Neuroscience, molecular biology, and the childhood roots of health disparities: Building a new framework for health promotion and disease prevention. *JAMA, 301*(21), 2252–59.

Simms, M. D., Dubowitz, H., & Szilagyi, M. A. (2000). Health care needs of children in the foster care system. *Pediatrics, 106* (Supplement 3), 909–18.

Sims, M., Sims, T. L., & Bruce, M. A. (2007). Urban poverty and infant mortality rate disparities. *Journal of the National Medical Association, 99*(4), 349–56.

Smeeding, T. M., & Waldfogel, J. (2010). Fighting poverty: Attentive policy can make a huge difference. *Journal of Policy Analysis and Management, 29*(2), 401–7.

Straus, M. A., & Gelles, R. J. (1986). Societal change and change in family violence from 1975 to 1985 as revealed by two national surveys. *Journal of Marriage and the Family*, 465–79.

U.S. Department of Health and Human Services. (2015). Head Start timeline. Administration for Children and Families, Early Childhood Learning and Knowledge Center, http://eclkc.ohs.acf.hhs.gov/hslc/hs/50th-anniversary /head-start-timeline

Waldfogel, J. (2000). What we know and don't know about the state of child protective service system and the links between poverty and child maltreatment. Remarks for Joint Center for Poverty Research Congressional Research Briefing on Child Welfare and Child Protection: Current Research and Policy Implications. Washington, DC, September 14.

———. (2010). *Tackling child poverty & improving child well-being: lessons from Britain*. First Focus.

Whipple, E. E., & Webster-Stratton, C. (1991). The role of parental stress in physically abusive families. *Child abuse & neglect, 15*(3), 279–91.

Wood, D. (2003). Effect of child and family poverty on child health in the United States. *Pediatrics, 112* (Supplement 3), 707–11.

Zuravin, S., & Greif, G. L. (1989). Normative and child-maltreating AFDC mothers. *Social Casework: The Journal of Contemporary Social Work, 74*, 76–84.

CHAPTER 11

Transforming Education

Toward Thinking Comprehensively About Education

Ezekiel J. Dixon-Román and Ama Nyame-Mensah

> We don't have after school programs when you
> don't want to do football, because that's pretty
> much the only thing that you can do in the
> inner-city . . . we're all thought of to be sports
> players. . . . Is there something else for us to do?
>
> —Dragon, *Rize*

This quote, from a youth in South Central Los Angeles in 2004, speaks to the ongoing inequality of educational opportunities outside of schooling. Socially and economically marginalized communities such as South Central Los Angeles are often bereft of out-of-school educational opportunities including quality early childhood educational centers, academic enrichment and tutoring programs, creative arts programs, dance classes, and career and technical education, to name just a few. What is equally as important yet not spoken to in Dragon's quote are the ecological conditions, mental and public health resources, and neighborhood safety that are also social determinants of child health and development. All of these more-than-schooling factors are critically important for the development of human capacities and successful navigation through the dominant institutions of society.

Dragon expresses not only the dearth of educational opportunities in his social reality but also his desire for something more. The "advantages" that Dragon desires are the everyday experiences of a broader understanding of education. This is an understanding of education that posits the process of education as much more comprehensive than schooling—a process that has only been enabled for those of the socially privileged spaces within society. This broader understanding of education, to which this chapter points toward, is what federal education policy has seemingly overlooked in its efforts involving school reform toward educational equity. In this chapter we argue that the national aims for educational equity will continue to be limited, with the narrow policy focus on school reform. We contend that in light of growing social science research on the importance of out-of-school influences on child health, learning, and development, there needs to be a transformation in federal policy on education. The United States needs federal policy on education that addresses the social policy concerns of out-of-school influences on the development of human capacities.

History of Education Policy in the United States and the Limits of School Reform

Federal education policy in the United States has traditionally focused its efforts on school reform. While the importance of schooling cannot be underscored enough, school reform efforts have rarely addressed the meaningful processes of complementary, supplementary, and comprehensive education that occur outside schools, in communities and the homes of learners. Further, these reform efforts have done little to support the academic achievement of students who live in socially and economically marginalized communities, where they inherit inequitable conditions and do not have access to an adequate and equitable education.

Despite the failures of school reform, in the past five decades there have been several instances where federal policy has supported complementary and supplementary schooling. This can be seen in the development and implementation of Head Start and breakfast and free/reduced lunch programs as well as through the expansion of supplemental educational services for poor performing schools under the No Child Left Behind Act of 2001. More recently, the Barack Obama administration has acknowledged the educative significance of complementary and supplementary education by developing the Promise Neighborhoods program and supporting the expansion of enrichment programs for before and after school through the 21st Century Community Learning Centers initiative. Although comprehensive education is not yet fully embraced in federal policy, recent reforms in education policy signal that there is a growing recognition that education is much more comprehensive than that which occurs in the four walls of a school.

Thinking Comprehensively About Education

Thinking comprehensively about education recognizes simultaneously the relevance and limitations of schooling. While schools continue to be an important institution of education in which learning takes place, comprehensive education affirms and acknowledges both the multiplicity of knowledge and ways of knowing as well as the legitimated knowledge of dominant institutions. This notion, however, requires that we understand education to be a social process that is ubiquitous in the various spaces and practices in society—not just in schools.

As such, what are some of the forms of supplementary and comprehensive education? Cremin (2007) and others (Gordon, Bridglall, & Meroe 2005; Varenne, Gordon, & Lin, 2009) have suggested that supplementary and comprehensive education might include, among many others, spaces and practices such as libraries, museums, child care centers, health education and clinics; martial arts, hip-hop, and afterschool programs; athletics; parenting practice workshops;

financial literacy programs; and prenatal services. It is through each of these institutions, programs, and practices that comprehensive and relational forms of equitable pedagogical experiences are enabled. These various forms of comprehensive education have substantial effects on educational outcomes and benefits to society.

Many studies (Durlak, Weissberg, & Pachan 2010; Hirsch, Deutsch, & DuBois, 2011; Hirsch, Hedges, Stawicki, & Mekinda, 2011; Mahoney, Vandell, Simpkins, & Zarrett, 2009) have documented the benefits of out-of-school programs and processes. Some of the evidence suggests that such programs have positive impacts on students' academic achievement (Durlak, Weissberg, & Pachan, 2010; Mahoney, Vandell, Simpkins, & Zarrett, 2009), youth development, and behaviors (Hirsch, Deutsch, & DuBois, 2011; Hirsch, Hedges, Stawicki, & Mekinda, 2011). Other work (Heckman, 2008) has estimated that investing in these types of programs early, such as high-quality early childhood education, yields a 7–10% per year return on investment to society. In fact, Heckman (2012) states "Short-term costs are more than offset by the immediate and long-term benefits through reduction in the need for special education and remediation, better health outcomes, reduced need for social services, lower criminal justice costs and increased self-sufficiency and productivity among families" (2). All of these findings point to the importance of out-of-school factors in influencing equity in human learning and development. Therefore, a public policy framework and agenda of comprehensive education is necessary in order to affirm and further enable the national goals of educational equity, particularly in the socially, racially, and economically marginalized spaces of society.

Given the marginality of many communities in the United States and the large magnitude of inequality in resources between communities (Massey & Denton, 1993; Quillian, 2007; Reardon & Bischoff, 2011; Sampson, Sharkey, & Raudenbush, 2008; Sharkey, 2008; Wilson, 1987), many children and youths grow up in marginalized communities where they inherit inequitable conditions, thus making equitable education an impossibility. These inequitable conditions include growing up in conditions of racism and discrimination, sexism, unemployment, financial stress, and lack of health insurance and residing in racially and classed-segregated neighborhoods that lack essential institutions such as supermarkets and have a high incidence of gun violence, high rates of unemployment, poor-quality schools, low rates of home ownership, high rates of incarceration, and high levels of ecological toxins. If we do not pay attention to and address the reproduced inequality of neighborhood resources and opportunities for comprehensive education, the national endeavors of educational excellence and equity will continue to be curtailed, and the children of the United States will continue to be left behind in the global community, a consequence the nation cannot afford.

Two Examples

A few examples will help illustrate how a policy agenda of comprehensive education that provides a host of services to meet the social, economic, and education needs of a community might be structured. While the Harlem Children's Zone is one of the most nationally recognized comprehensive education models upon which other initiatives have been designed, we would like to highlight alternative promising models so as to demonstrate that comprehensive education cannot be encompassed by a singular model but instead has to be developed in a way that is responsive to community needs and culture. The first example is the Jacobs Center for Neighborhood Innovation (JCNI) in San Diego, California (Clark & Bryan, 2012), and the second is the Broader Bolder Approach (BBA) to school reform in Newark, New Jersey (Wells & Noguera, 2012). Both initiatives attempt to address the need for comprehensive wraparound social, economic, health, and educational services for educational equity.

The Jacobs Center for Neighborhood Innovation

The Diamond Neighborhoods of Southeastern San Diego, California, are home to more than 88,000 residents. The Diamond

Neighborhoods are primarily Hispanic (43%) and African American (30%) with significant Caucasian (11%) and Asian (11%) populations as well as smaller populations of Somalis, Samoans, Sudanese, Laotians, and Chamorro. Close to 60% of the population is non-English speaking, with over 20% of residents' incomes falling below the poverty line. Almost 40% of the region's residents are under age 18, making youths a key target population in this community.

Over the last several decades, the Diamond Neighborhoods have experienced physical, economic, and academic decline. In an attempt to revitalize the Diamond Neighborhoods, the JCNI—a local nonprofit foundation—partnered with the residents of the area and created a long-term comprehensive community development plan to improve the social well-being of the community. The community development plan included two core components: (1) economic investment and (2) support for community-led social initiatives including youth development, health, and education programs.

In recent years, support for youth-led initiatives has continued to be a primary goal of the JCNI. The JCNI's trademark listening strategy guiding community development efforts led the director of the Community Building Department, Roque Barros, to ask the residents themselves, "What should our relationships with youth look like? What youth projects are already in existence that we can support?" Resident responses led the JCNI to provide support to a neighborhood Teen Center and the Writerz Blok Urban Arts Park. Significant time and technical resources were also devoted to supporting the organizational development of two existing community-run educational nonprofits, the Elementary Institute of Science, a summer and after-school science enrichment program, and a Pazzaz Educational Enrichment Center, a local after-school tutoring group.

All of this and more have contributed to the development of a comprehensive educational system within the heart of the Diamond Neighborhoods. For further information on the JCNI's transformative work in the Diamond Neighborhoods, please see Andrea Yoder Clark and Tracey Bryan's chapter in *Thinking Comprehensively About Education* (2012).

The Broader Bolder Approach

The BBA is a strategy that aims to transform schools in Newark, New Jersey, through the development of civic capacity. Stone et al. (2001) and others (Noguera, 2003; Orr, 2007) have defined civic capacity as the creation of a series of strategic partnerships between schools, businesses, universities, hospitals, local government, and a broad array of neighborhood-based service organizations. Such partnerships are designed to increase local support for schools and enhance the social capital of students and their families. Policy advocates of civic capacity building have argued that providing schools with substantial increases in external support is the most cost-effective means for delivering the resources and support they need. The theory holds that such support will lead to greater accountability, better functioning schools, and higher levels of student achievement.

The BBA is an ambitious reform project that has been launched as an attempt to develop a comprehensive school reform strategy that will address issues and challenges arising out of the distressed social contexts in which families and public schools are situated through a variety of school-based interventions. The BBA model includes social service provisions, economic development, and civic engagement with school reform efforts in order to ensure that efforts to transform schools are not undermined by environmental hardships or the lack of quality control attention in educational practices and interventions. The central goals of the BBA are to expand learning opportunities for students by investing in quality early childhood education, extend the traditional school day, and enrich the curriculum by providing an education that is relevant to the economic, political, cultural, and social life of the 21st century.

As is true in many other high poverty urban areas, a combination of social, economic, and political problems has historically constrained efforts to improve schools in Newark, New Jersey. These problems are also at the root of many of the current challenges confronting its residents. The BBA strategy seeks to mitigate the detrimental effects of the environment by developing the capacity of schools to respond to student needs and by drawing on support and resources from local institutions.

The BBA strategy also seeks to transform the way urban public schools typically serve low-income children of color and their families. The BBA uses data to carefully monitor student progress and the ways programs are implemented to be more responsive to the social and educational needs of children and their families. The goal is to respond immediately to evidence that programs are not implemented with fidelity or are not achieving the goals that have been set.

For further information on the BBA to school reform in Newark, New Jersey, please see Lauren Wells and Pedro Noguera's chapter in *Thinking Comprehensively About Education* (2012).

Concluding Remarks: Toward Comprehensive Education Policy as National Imperative

In their compelling paper, Gordon and Heincke (2012) argue that there are limits to what schools can do alone and what can be achieved through school reform. They call for the need to push for a national program and a federal office of affirmative development of intellective competence that focus on better enabling communities and families to support the academic and personal development of children from preconception through college. Based on the recommendations of the National Study Group on Supplementary/ Comprehensive Education, they provide a framework for a public policy agenda on comprehensive education that would achieve the national endeavors of social and academic equity and excellence. They argue that these national endeavors are not plausibly attainable from school reform efforts alone. It is our contention that the aims and endeavors toward educational equity can only be achieved comprehensively.

This chapter considers the implications to public policy based on a comprehensive transformation of education. A public policy framework and agenda of comprehensive education is necessary in order to affirm and further enable the comprehensive systems and practices of education in society at large and in socially and economically marginalized communities in particular. This is an imperative if the democratic aims of the United States are to address the non-democratic reality of social inequality and educational inequity. If we don't transform education in the United States and pay particular attention to and address the reproduced inequality of opportunities for comprehensive education, the national endeavors of educational excellence and equity will continue to be compromised, and the children of the United States will continue to be left behind in the global community, a consequence that this nation cannot afford.

Sources

Clark, A. Y., & Bryan, T. (2012). San Diego's Diamond Neighborhoods and the Jacobs Center for Neighborhood Innovation. In Ezekiel Dixon-Román & Edmund W. Gordon (Eds.), *Thinking Comprehensively About Education: Spaces of Educative Possibility and Their Implications for Public Policy*. New York: Routledge.

Cremin, L. (2007). Public education and the education of the public. *Teachers College Record, 109*(7), 1545–58. (Original work published 1975.)

Durlak, J. A., Weissberg, R. P., & Pachan, M. A. (2010). Meta-analysis of after-school programs that seek to promote personal and social skills in children and adolescents. *American Journal of Community Psychology, 46*, 294–309.

Gordon, E. W., Bridglall, B. L., & Meroe, A. S. (2005). *Supplementary education: The hidden curriculum of high academic achievement*. Lanham, MD: Rowman & Littlefield.

Gordon, E. W., & Heincke, P. (2012). School reform: A limited strategy in national education policy. In Ezekiel Dixon-Román & Edmund W. Gordon (Eds.), *Thinking comprehensively about education*. New York: Routledge.

Heckman, J. (2008). Schools, skills, and synapses. *Economic Inquiry, 46*(3), 289–324.

———. (2012). *Invest in early childhood development: Reduce deficits, strengthen the economy*. https://docs.google.com/viewerng/viewer?url=www.heckman

equation.org/sites/default/files/F_HeckmanDeficitPieceCUSTOM -Generic_052714.pdf

Hirsch, B. J., Deutsch, N., & DuBois, D. (2011). *After-school centers and youth development: Case studies of success and failure.* New York: Cambridge University Press.

Hirsch, B. J., Hedges, L. V., Stawicki, J., & Mekinda, M. (2011). *After-school programs for high school students: An evaluation of after school matters.* Technical Report.

Mahoney, J. L., Vandell, D. L., Simpkins, S. D., & Zarrett, N. R. (2009). Adolescent out-of-school activities. In Richard M. Lerner & Lauren Steinberg (Eds.), *Handbook of adolescent psychology,* Vol. 2: *Contextual influences on adolescent development* (3rd ed.), pp. 228–67. Hoboken, NJ: Wiley.

Massey, D. S., & Denton, N. A. (1993). *American apartheid: Segregation and the making of the underclass.* Cambridge, MA: Harvard University Press.

Noguera, P. (2003). *City schools and the American dream: Reclaiming the promise of public education.* New York: Teachers College Press.

Orr, M. (2007). *Transforming the city: Community organizing the challenge of political change.* Lawrence: University of Kansas Press.

Quillian, L. (2007). Does segregation create winners and losers? Education and spatial segregation on the basis of income and race. Paper presented at the Annual Meeting of the Population Association of America.

Reardon, S., & Bischoff, K. (2011). Income inequality and income segregation. *American Journal of Sociology, 116*(4) (January), 1092–53.

Sampson, R. J., Sharkey, P., & Raudenbush, S. W. (2008). Durable effects of concentrated disadvantage on verbal ability among African-American children. *Proceedings of the National Academy of Sciences, 105*(3), 845–52.

Sharkey, Patrick. (2008). The intergenerational transmission of context. *American Journal of Sociology, 113,* 931–69.

Stone, C., Henig, J., Jones, B., & Pierannunzi, C. (2001). Building civic capacity: The politics of reforming urban schools. Lawrence: University of Kansas Press.

Varenne, H., Gordon, E. W., & Lin, L. (2009). *Theoretical perspectives on comprehensive education: The way forward.* Perspectives on Comprehensive Education Series 2. Lewiston, NY: Edwin Mellen.

Wells, L., & Noguera, P. (2012). A broader and bolder approach for Newark. In Ezekiel Dixon-Román & Edmund W. Gordon (Eds.), *Thinking comprehensively about education.* New York: Routledge.

Wilson, W. J. (1987). *The truly disadvantaged: The inner city, the underclass, and public policy.* Chicago: University of Chicago Press.

CHAPTER 12

From Poverty to Well-Being

New Tools for Addressing Concentrated Disadvantage

Mark J. Stern

In a nation so committed to success and affluence, it is not surprising that the topic of poverty gets short shrift in the United States. This lack of attention has influenced how we measure poverty as well. The official poverty line was flawed when it was developed a half century ago. Yet it has remained largely unchanged even as the gap has widened between poverty statistics and the realities of poor Americans. Because poverty is measured by Americans' capacity to consume, an updated poverty measure would still ignore other dimensions of individual well-being and in the process neglect how nonfinancial assets of poor communities can be mobilized to improve their quality of life.

Why We Need a New Poverty Measure

The official poverty line has a real-world impact on poor people's lives. Many federal grants (such as Community Development Block Grants) and assistance to individuals and families (including food

stamps, now called Supplemental Nutritional Assistance, and housing subsidies) are tied to it. Yet in the half century since it was developed, the official poverty line has become a less accurate indicator
of economic need.

The poverty line was created somewhat accidentally. Mollie
Orshansky, who is credited as its inventor, was trying to get a better
handle on child poverty at the Social Security Administration at the
same time that President Lyndon Johnson was mobilizing the nation
for his war on poverty. Johnson's aides realized that if they were
going to fight a war on poverty, they needed a way to know when
it was won. Orshansky's work—which adjusted poverty for family
size, the number of children, and several other factors—provided
a good starting point for estimating the prevalence of need. Within
a few years, however, its flaws became obvious. By 1968, in fact, the
federal government was ready to abandon the Orshansky line, but
bureaucratic inertia saved it.

What is wrong with the official poverty measure? At its core,
it equates welfare with the ability to consume. In other words, it is
driven by whether a household has sufficient income to pay for a
standard market basket of goods. The measure compares a standard
of income adequacy (the poverty line) to estimates of individual and
family income. It does both poorly. The standard has its origins in a
19th-century idea that a poor family is one who spends more than a
third of its income on food. Orshansky took this idea and combined
it with a government estimate of food costs from the mid-1950s.

The poverty standard, then, has been obsolete since it was *first*
calculated in the 1960s. Housing and health care, two major elements
of today's family budget, did not figure in the 1960s calculation. A
more accurate standard would include these and other expenses and
thus push the poverty rate higher. The estimate of income is flawed
as well because it ignores the role of noncash assistance (think Medi-
care, housing subsidies, and food stamps) and the tax system (think
Earned Income Tax Credit [EITC]). A more accurate measure of
income would tend to push the poverty rate lower.

Since the 1980s at least, the search for a better standard has been
bogged down in politics. The Ronald Reagan administration tried to

demonstrate that there was no more poverty in America by boosting income estimates while holding the standard constant. Later, Reagan abandoned this approach and told the nation that we had fought a war on poverty, and "poverty won." During the 1990s, the National Academy of Science commissioned a special report on improving the poverty measure, but Republicans in Congress refused to consider its adoption.

In 2009, President Barack Obama's first census director, Rebecca Blank, sidestepped the partisan fights by having her agency develop a supplemental poverty measure (SPM) that sits beside the official measure. The SPM, which incorporates most of the recommendations to improve the measure since the 1990s, changes our understanding of the extent and distribution of poverty. Overall, the SPM estimates poverty at about one percentage point higher in 2013 than the official poverty rate. Just as important, it changes our understanding of who is poor. The giant gap between the poverty rate of children and older Americans identified by the official poverty line is narrowed by the SPM. In addition, the poverty rate of African Americans drops significantly, while that of Hispanics increases. Furthermore, the SPM changes our entire narrative about consumption poverty. Whereas the official poverty line suggests that we have made practically no progress in reducing poverty since the 1970s, the SPM—by taking into consideration changes in the tax system (especially the EITC) and the expansion of noncash benefits—shows that government policy since that time has been effective in reducing poverty.

Beyond Consumption

Although the SPM is a great improvement in measuring the inability of many Americans to achieve an adequate level of consumption, it shares with the official poverty line a fundamental limitation. Both have their origins in the 19th-century idea that the core measure of human well-being is an adequate level of personal consumption. For an era when scarcity was still the norm, this standard made complete sense. But since the middle of the 20th century, we have come to appreciate that this one-dimensional conception of welfare ignores many of the major changes in how people think about "a good life." The civil rights movement taught us that human dignity and a life free from social exclusion and the stigma of difference are goals worth fighting for. From the environmental movement, we have learned that individual consumption is tarnished if the quality of our surroundings is despoiled. Finally, the emerging debate over social and economic inequality in regard to the publication of Thomas Piketty's *Capital in the Twenty-First Century* suggests that the exploding gap between rich and poor affects our lives as much as the amount of income we have to spend.

These new ideas about a good life are changing the discussion of how we measure well-being. Without abandoning the importance of income and adequate consumption, contemporary research focuses on the many dimensions constituting human well-being.

Much of this innovative work traces its origins back to the *capabilities approach*, associated with philosopher Martha Nussbaum and economist Amartya Sen. This approach starts with a simple question: What conditions are necessary for humans to live a life they have reason to value? Yet the answer to this question is far from simple. Certainly, a life free from hunger and want is part of it, but the inquiry moves beyond material conditions. A decent environment, social affiliation, and opportunities for recreation and leisure (not in the sense of idleness but in the older meaning of time for contemplation and discourse) are all part of the answer. Most challenging, the capabilities approach includes both public policy and how people live their private lives. Nussbaum has been particularly concerned with the role of private intimidation and limits on people imposed by sexism and racism. By the same token, social policy may facilitate social integration, but developing a sense of trust and belonging in a community ultimately rests upon nongovernmental interactions between people.

How do these ideas fit into the current poverty debate? Imagine two low-income communities with official poverty rates twice the national average. In one community, however, the mobilization of private and public resources has improved the public environment (more trees and public spaces), improved the health of the population (reduced obesity, hypertension, and low birth weights), and increased the sense of trust and belonging among residents, while in the other this hasn't happened. Although both communities would still struggle against the limits of economic opportunity, the chances of living a life they have reason to value is much higher in the first community. So improved well-being makes a difference, even if it doesn't necessarily reduce the poverty rate.

Translating these philosophical ideas into data and metrics is a tall order. European and international organizations have taken the lead in expanding new ways of thinking about well-being. The developed welfare states of Western and Northern Europe, on the one hand, have reduced consumption poverty. At the same time, these countries have illuminated processes of *social exclusion* in which low attachment to the labor force is often reinforced by ethnic differences and geographic isolation—a situation highlighted by the riots in French housing estates in 2005.

More recently, a number of international organizations have sponsored studies of social justice and well-being based on *multi-dimensional* models. For example, the Organisation for Economic Cooperation and Development (OECD) rated its member nations on dimensions ranging from poverty to labor market inclusion, educational access, and intergenerational equity.

The most influential effort to develop a multidimensional index of well-being is the French government's Commission on the Measurement of Economic Performance and Social Progress, coauthored by Joseph Stiglitz, Amartya Sen, and Jean-Paul Fitoussi (2009). The report spells out eight dimensions of well-being and provides specific recommendations regarding what social conditions should be included in each (Table 1). In addition to assessing the average condition of a population on each dimension, the report emphasizes that a measure of well-being must be mindful of inequality across all dimensions. This point suggests that we should take into account *concentrations of advantage and disadvantage*, where the same populations are consistently very low or very high on the various dimensions.

Table 1. Dimensions of social well-being./Source: Stiglitz, Sen, & Fitoussi (2009).

i.	Material living standards (income, consumption, and wealth)
ii.	Health
iii.	Education
iv.	Personal activities, including work
v.	Political voice and governance
vi.	Social connections and relationships
vii.	Environment (present and future conditions)
viii.	Insecurity, economic as well as of a physical nature

These international efforts to move beyond poverty share many positive features as well as a common shortcoming. Virtually all of the studies have focused on rating *nations* across the various dimensions. As a result—in contrast to their theoretical origins—they focus almost exclusively on labor markets and public policy rather than the many elements of a life outside of these sectors that we have "reason to value." More so, a focus on national data makes it impossible to identify the specific populations and places where disadvantage or advantage is most common.

A Neighborhood-Based Measure of Social Well-Being

My research team—composed of the Social Impact of the Arts Project at the University of Pennsylvania and the Reinvestment Fund, a community development financial institution—combine the insights of the capabilities approach with empirical social well-being studies to develop a *neighborhood-based measure of social well-being* for Philadelphia. By doing so, we broaden the international framework to include public, civic, and private contributors to well-being. Given the extensive data on concentrated disadvantage, we simultaneously identify parts of the city with poor opportunities on multiple measures as well as places that face a number of challenges but have potential sources of strength. Finally, the neighborhood-based measure allows us to identify potential strategies for the alleviation of poverty and social exclusion for which both national and local efforts are appropriate.

Our research team faced a number of empirical challenges in undertaking the project. First, the set of dimensions outlined by Stiglitz, Sen, and Fitoussi (2009) have to be adapted to a neighborhood-level measure. We found that income, labor force participation, and educational attainment are so closely correlated that it makes no sense to treat them as separate dimensions. By the same token, social connection and health, rather than emerging as single dimensions, break into two or three distinct elements.

We were also challenged in finding sources of data. Only three of the eventual dimensions are based primarily on national government data—economic well-being, housing burden, and economic and ethnic diversity. We found most of the data from nonprofits and local government sources, ranging from city agency reports of confirmed cases of child abuse and neglect to satellite imagery of land use and infrared radiation.

In the final analysis, we identify 13 dimensions of well-being (Table 2). Economic well-being, closest to a traditional poverty measure, remains an important element of the index and is correlated with several dimensions—including school effectiveness, social stress (high teen births, deaths by homicide, cases of child abuse and neglect), and security (crime rates, reports of neighborhood disputes).

Other elements of the index pick up dimensions of well-being largely missed by the traditional focus on and measure of poverty. Face-to-face social connection includes data on levels of trust, belonging, and neighborhood organizational participation. The environment factor includes measures of green space and excessive summer heat. Our housing index identifies neighborhoods with excessive cost burdens and overcrowding, elements that are only partially correlated with a standard measure of poverty or income (Figure 1).

Once we completed our neighborhood-based index of social well-being for Philadelphia, we then identified parts of the city scoring consistently high or low across all measures. Because economic well-being is correlated with school effectiveness, social stress,

Table 2. Dimensions of well-being and included variables.

Dimension	Subindexes	Description
Economic well-being		Material standard of living: income, educational attainment, labor force participation
Economic and ethnic diversity		Income inequality, household income diversity, ethnic diversity (percent of residents not members of largest ethnic group)
School effectiveness		Current school proficiency scores, dropout rate, private school attendance
Housing burden		Overcrowding, housing financial stress, distance from work
Social connection	Institutional	Nonprofit organizations, geographic mobility
	Face-to-face connection	Trust, belonging, participation
	Cultural asset index	Nonprofit and for-profit cultural providers, resident artists, cultural participants
Security		High personal and property crime rates, Human Relations Commission complaints
Health	Personal health	Diabetes, hypertension, overall health condition, obesity
	Insurance, access	Low insurance rates, delayed care due to cost, use of ER
	Social stress	High teen pregnancy, lack of prenatal care, high homicide, reports of child abuse and neglect
Environment		Parks, trees, grass, underground streams (inverse), heat vulnerability
Political voice		Percent of eligible population casting ballots in 2010 and 2012

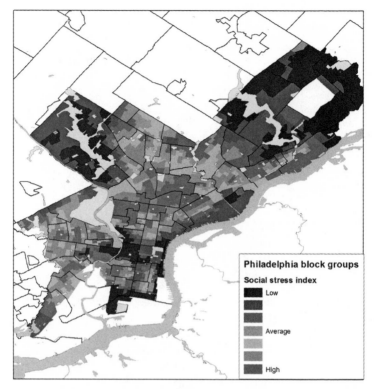

Figure 1. Social stress index.

personal health, and security, parts of the city with concentrated
disadvantage and concentrated advantage reflect these factors.

Yet even among neighborhoods with concentrated disadvantage, we find dimensions of strength (Figure 2). The Ogontz/Belfield
neighborhood in North Philadelphia, for example, has low economic
well-being, poor school effectiveness, and high crime. Yet our estimates suggest that its residents have above average face-to-face social
connection, tied to a higher than average level of trust and community participation. Likewise, East Germantown suffers from a host of
disadvantages but also shows strength in its environmental amenities.

The balance of weakness and strength is even clearer in many of
the mixed neighborhoods, which show a concentration of neither

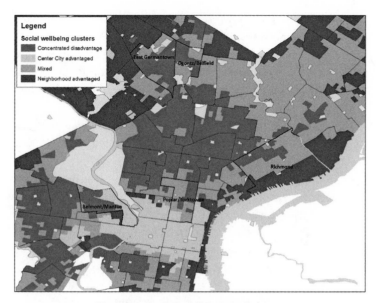

Figure 2. Social well-being clusters.

disadvantages nor advantages. For example, Richmond along the Delaware River has a host of challenges, but school effectiveness is above average in the neighborhood. The Poplar/Yorktowne neighborhood, just north of Center City, scores low on many factors but high on both institutional connection and cultural assets.

Leveraging Well-Being for Community Change

Since the 1960s, national and local leaders have sponsored a variety of strategies for reducing poverty and improving the quality of life in urban neighborhoods. Yet the tools used to identify neighborhoods for intervention make it difficult to tailor strategies to a neighborhood's unique qualities. Although local actions may mitigate social conditions, local government can do little to reduce the official poverty rate among neighborhood residents. In fact, this second realization motivated the Michael Bloomberg administration in New York

City to develop its own poverty measure. It became clear that many of the city's antipoverty initiatives—for example, expanding the proportion of eligible residents who applied for the EITC—would have no effect on its official poverty rate. The Bill de Blasio administration has expanded this strategy with a renewed focus on neighborhood disparities across the city's five boroughs.

The Obama administration's Promise Zone initiative—although starved for resources by Congress—has sought to incorporate other aspects of well-being by requiring applicants to identify neighborhood assets. The West Philadelphia Promise Zone in the Belmont and Mantua neighborhoods, it turns out, scores high according to our measures of institutional social connection (concentration of nonprofits), political voice (voter participation), and environmental amenities (green space, parks)—assets that could serve as building blocks for neighborhood renewal.

In the coming years, we are more likely to see local efforts targeting disadvantage rather than a sweeping national campaign. These local efforts may do little to change the official poverty rate but nevertheless increase the overall social well-being of urban communities. Only national labor market conditions—increasing job growth and declining unemployment—and the expansion of government cash assistance will move the official rate. In contrast, an index of social well-being provides the starting point for a host of local initiatives. Identifying ways that existing social connections and institutional networks can be leveraged to improve schools or reduce crime are examples of how local attention may reap local rewards. Moving from poverty to social well-being provides us with a new framework for understanding a neighborhood's assets and liabilities and using assets to enhance the quality of life and opportunities for all residents.

Sources

Gasper, D. (1997). Sen's capability approach and Nussbaum's capabilities ethic. *Journal of International Development, 9*(2), 281–302.

Nussbaum, M. (2003). Capabilities as fundamental entitlements: Sen and social justice. *Feminist Economics, 9*(2–3), 33–59.

O'Connor, A. (2009). *Poverty knowledge: Social science, social policy, and the poor in twentieth-century U.S. history.* Princeton, NJ: Princeton University Press.

OECD. (2011). *Social justice in the OECD: How do the member states compare?* Gutersloh, Germany: Bertelsmann Stiftung.

Piketty, T. (2014). *Capital in the twenty-first century.* Cambridge, MA: Belknap Press of Harvard University Press.

Sen, A. 1992. *Inequality reexamined.* Cambridge, MA: Harvard University Press.

Short, K. (2014). The supplemental poverty measure: 2013. U.S. Bureau of the Census, Current Population.

Stiglitz, J., Sen, A., & Fitoussi, J. (2009). The measurement of economic performance and social progress revisited. *Reflections and Overview.* Commission on the Measurement of Economic Performance and Social Progress, Paris.

Wimer, C., Fox, L. E., Garfinkel, I., Kaushal, N., & Waldfogel, J. (2013). *Trends in poverty with an anchored supplemental poverty measure.* Institute for Research on Poverty, University of Wisconsin-Madison.

CONTRIBUTORS

Benjamin Chrisinger is a postdoctoral research fellow in Stanford University's School of Medicine.

Cindy W. Christian holds the Anthony A. Latini Endowed Chair in the Prevention of Child Abuse and Neglect and is a professor of pediatrics and the associate dean for admissions in the Perelman School of Medicine at the University of Pennsylvania.

Cynthia A. Connolly is an associate professor of nursing in the School of Nursing at the University of Pennsylvania.

Dennis P. Culhane is the Dana & Andrew Stone Chair in Social Policy in the School of Social Policy & Practice at the University of Pennsylvania.

Christina Denard is a doctoral candidate in social welfare in the School of Social Policy & Practice at the University of Pennsylvania.

Ezekiel J. Dixon-Román is an associate professor of social policy in the School of Social Policy & Practice at the University of Pennsylvania.

Malitta Engstrom is an assistant professor of social work in the School of Social Policy & Practice at the University of Pennsylvania.

Kara Finck is a practice associate professor of law and director of the Interdisciplinary Child Advocacy Clinic in the University of Pennsylvania Law School.

Nancy Franke is the director of the Goldring Reentry Initiative at the School of Social Policy & Practice at the University of Pennsylvania.

Antonio Garcia is an assistant professor of social work in the School of Social Policy & Practice at the University of Pennsylvania.

Toorjo Ghose is an associate professor of social work in the School of Social Policy & Practice at the University of Pennsylvania.

Johanna Greeson is an assistant professor of social work in the School of Social Policy & Practice at the University of Pennsylvania.

David Hemenway is a professor of health policy at Harvard University and the director of the Harvard Injury Control Research Center.

Amy Hillier is an associate professor in city and regional planning in the School of Design at the University of Pennsylvania and holds a secondary appointment in the School of Social Policy & Practice at the University of Pennsylvania.

Roberta Rehner Iversen is an associate professor of social work in the School of Social Policy & Practice at the University of Pennsylvania.

John L. Jackson, Jr. is the Richard Perry University Professor and the dean of the School of Social Policy & Practice at the University of Pennsylvania.

Ama Nyame-Mensah is a doctoral candidate in social welfare in the School of Social Policy & Practice at the University of Pennsylvania.

Phyllis Solomon is a professor of social work and the associate dean for research in the School of Social Policy & Practice at the University of Pennsylvania.

Susan B. Sorenson is a professor of social policy and the director of the Evelyn Jacobs Ortner Center on Family Violence in the School of Social Policy & Practice at the University of Pennsylvania.

Mark J. Stern is the Kenneth L. M. Pray Professor of Social Policy and History in the School of Social Policy & Practice at the University of Pennsylvania. He also codirects the Urban Studies Program in the School of Arts and Sciences.

Allison Thompson is a doctoral candidate in social welfare in the School of Social Policy & Practice at the University of Pennsylvania.

Alexandra Wimberly is a doctoral candidate in social welfare in the School of Social Policy & Practice at the University of Pennsylvania.

Debra Schilling Wolfe is the founding executive director of the Field Center for Children's Policy, Practice & Research, a School of Social Policy & Practice collaboration with the University of Pennsylvania School of Law, Perelman School of Medicine, and School of Nursing and with the Children's Hospital of Philadelphia.